Is Anybod ....

The Urbana Free Library

To renew materials call
217-367-4057

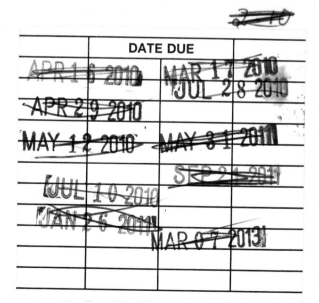

About The Author

A former professional musician, both teacher and performer, Mary Bowmaker has always loved writing, small successes over the years encouraging and inspiring her to write her first book *A Little School on the Downs*, a record of the life and work of a headmistress and her school in Victorian England.

Is anybody there..., a book recording true experiences of the paranormal, is a subject close to her heart since childhood when she listened to the experiences of grown-ups and especially her grandmother who was a natural medium. Since then, her love and interest in the subject has blossomed into serious research which has become the most fulfilling part of her life, along with her desire to pass on to others great truths and experiences which should be told.

Mary Bowmaker lives in the North of England and in contrast to her 'spiritual' pursuits is her enthusiastic participation in physical activities such as walking, kick-boxing and power yoga.

Is Anybody There...

by

Mary Bowmaker

ORDINARY PEOPLE AND

TRUE PARANORMAL EXPERIENCES

COURTENBEDE

2 -1 0

17 -

Contents

This book is dedicated to my beloved husband
Peter R Bowmaker

'Even though you're gone, we're still a team.'

List of illustrations

Acknowledgements

My thanks to:

The Religious Experience Research Centre, otherwise known as the RERC, University of Wales, Lampeter, Ceredigion. The RERC does such a marvellous job in receiving and anonymously archiving accounts of experience from members of the public, and making them available to researchers. Special thanks to Anne Watkins, MA, and Dr Wendy Dossett, who looked after me, having time and patience for this would-be researcher who found her way to their door. Jane Tatam from Amolibros has been splendid in her appreciation of the subject and kindly understanding at all times during this 'project'. Thank you, Jane and Amolibros for 'being there'.

The Photographic Department of the University of Newcastle Upon Tyne was always helpful and willing to assist when I sought advice.

To friends and acquaintances who helped me by advising, passing on material, discussing, listening, and for having faith in what I was attempting to do.

My grateful and humble thanks to all those who so generously and trustingly gave of their stories, their experiences – such a private part of their lives, and without whose contribution this book would not have been written. My grateful thanks for the photographs; and to Norah and Kathleen who stood with me at a sad time, thank you.

Mary Bowmaker

IS ANYBODY THERE...

'Is anybody there...' Those words resonate with my first meeting with Mary Bowmaker in early 1984. Mary had applied to study with me for a Master's degree in Drama as Education at the University of Newcastle-Upon-Tyne.

Her first book, *A Little School on the Downs*, a true record of the work of Harriet Finlay Johnson, head teacher who lived in Victorian England, metamorphosed from her successful thesis. Harriet Finlay Johnson made her presence felt in many ways both leading up to, and during the research of her work. Through it, Mary Bowmaker and I were on our way to a rich teaching collaboration and a sharing of our mutual sense of 'the invisible'. I am proud to have shared this experience with Mary and the 'invisible presence' which at other times and in other places I have been privileged to encounter. I am delighted that Mary's sensitivity to the unseen has enabled others' experiences to be collected between these covers so that those of like mind can extend their understanding of glimpses of possible 'anybody's being there'.

Dr Dorothy Heathcote, author and former senior lecturer in
Education at the University of Newcastle-upon-Tyne

Whatever nationality or creed, this book will make the reader more heedful of their own, perhaps previously untapped, inner knowledge, and signs often dismissed as fanciful. Through the book you will find yourself stimulated by the wonder and mystery of a new awareness: an awareness of the inter-flowing nature of this beautiful world and of the world beyond. You will become aware of what 'love' can achieve. A 'must' read to help understand the unexplained.

Sylvia Povey Kennedy BA(Hons) – Training & Education. Fellow of the International Federation of Reflexologists

Names that are fictitious are to protect the privacy of the contributor.

Foreword by William Roache, MBE

OF COURSE THERE IS more to life than that perceived by our five senses. Most of us at some time have experienced the inexplicable. My own interest in things beyond was stimulated by two fears: the fear of death and of infinity. There had to be more to life than this physical existence, and infinity is beyond our understanding.

We must always seek the truth, but to find the truth, we sometimes have to overcame our own opinions and beliefs. It is a hard road. The more we understand about other realms the easier it becomes.

Books like *Is anybody there...* by Mary Bowmaker, help us as we walk along the path to greater understanding. It is also a great joy to read.

William Roache, MBE

Introduction

I SUPPOSE THERE HAS to be a compelling reason for wanting to write a book. You either have a fascination for a subject, or a depth of knowledge you are keen to pass on to others, or a thirst for research of one sort or another; perhaps there is a tale to tell, or simply a desire to chronicle extraordinary events.

All my life I have been aware of help and guidance from, to quote Professor Sir Alister Hardy FRS *'this unnamed something'*[1] most of us refer to as 'God'. And being aware of this 'help and guidance' and having met or read about countless others who have also been aware (of this), I decided to record some of the experiences. Some of them have been told to me personally, over many years; some I have received by letter or have pursued through research; a few are my own. Mainly evidenced in the intricate web of the so-called 'paranormal', the idea that these experiences are for a select few is totally false. The 'unnamed something', the 'universal energy', the 'life force', 'God', is there for each one of us.

That there is a spiritual reawakening taking place in our world (not in spite of all the turmoil around but perhaps *because* of it), there is apparently little doubt. Recently we have seen many demonstrations against war; prayers for peace (even at yoga classes); a turn to alternate remedies, including healing and meditation. (At a wedding, during the reception, a Tibetan bell was struck for silence and to allow the guests time to contemplate and to meditate.) To quote a reporter in *The Sunday Times*, *'we may not be getting our spiritual fix in church any more but if the growth in "spirit oriented" practices like yoga are anything to go by, our hunger is greater than ever.'*

This book is not about religious dogma or creed in any shape or form. It is about lives – the lives of ordinary people who, for one reason or another, have been touched by this 'unnamed something'. It is about their experiences – experiences that could happen to any one of us at any time, any place, but we would need to know how to interpret these experiences should they happen. We would need to know how to understand them, relate to them and, hopefully, through them, be able to accept without a shadow of doubt the reality that, in our need, there is a power that transcends all earthly power on which we can call.

In the present turmoil and uncertainty of our world, an upsurge of interest in new age religions brings with it an unprecedented acceptance of healing, alternate remedies, yoga and many other forms of self-help. (A top scientist has recently given his backing to astrology, asserting that the movements of the stars 'can influence us' after all.) There is a new seeking, a deep longing, for more than our material world can offer. There is a longing for 'meaning'. That strange experiences, interpreting visions and dreams, visiting mediums and so on, are recent innovations, is of course untrue. Such things have always been 'there', but in certain past generations have been mainly shunned, ignored, and definitely not openly discussed. Today the climate of change has heralded a new open-mindedness; a questioning, that is both refreshing and necessary for our understanding. And part of that understanding is perhaps to realise that many, even most of the strange occurrences that happen in life may seem ordinary, even trivial, to the non-participant. But to the recipient they could mean everything.

How have we ourselves reacted to something 'strange' that

must have happened at least once in our lives? Were we quick to say 'imagination', 'coincidence', 'just one of those things'? Or did we pause, and think; ponder, and wonder; allowing our minds the freedom to explore the possibility of maybe a deeper meaning?

The French philosopher and mathematician, Blaise Pascal, said that authors who talk about their work as 'my book', 'my history' or 'my commentary' would be better to say 'our book', 'our history' or 'our commentary' as their writings contain as much of the thoughts of other authors as their own.[2] In trying to take Pascal's theory a stage further, can we move forward together in this work realising that if stories overlap and could have been included in any one of the following chapters, it is because they have more than one message to impart? Can we move forward together pooling our thoughts and energies, exploring and decoding experiences; experiences that are often, as has been already mentioned, so ordinary, so down to earth that we will be incredulous at their simplicity, yet moved by the depth of their meaning? There are experiences that, looked at in a new light, with new eyes and with new understanding, we might be able to say of them, 'Yes, I too was there.' Other experiences might be too fanciful for our digestion, too up in the clouds to accept. But in reading the many and varied stories, can we remind ourselves to have respect for the teller? They have shared with us what is to many, a most private part of their lives – stories which, but for a desire to help mankind in its search for the truth, might never have been told.

As for me, I am just the chronicler, the reporter, the relater, a raconteur of experiences, teller of tales. Truthful tales, fascinating tales, hopeful, often mysterious...but it is together that we will view them, study them, and it is together that we will pose the question, '*Is* anybody there?'

Chapter One

'Something ordinary happening, on an ordinary day, in ordinary life, yet there was something that made it seem 'special'. When people have a paranormal experience, they know they have had one.'

THE SUMMER HOLIDAY NOW over, the two families waited patiently at the airport for the plane home. Everything had gone according to plan, the whole holiday a success, including the sharing of a big house in Spain. The house had an old part and a new part, the new part housing a play-room; ideal for their four young children.

Sitting in the airport lounge reflecting on it all, the parents quizzed the children, 'You didn't seem to use the playroom, why didn't you?' Suddenly the whole atmosphere of carefree happiness changed as they froze on the spot at the reply: 'Because it was full with the other children; they didn't want us.'

As far as the parents were concerned, there were no other children in the house, but they also knew that their little ones would not, could not, invent such a story.

Later, at home, Geoff confessed to the hairs on his arms 'standing up' as he gently questioned his young daughter about the 'other children', going icy cold at her nonchalant reply. 'A little Spanish girl often came and sat on my bed talking to me.'

The fact that the experience of seeing 'spirit children' in the playroom was accepted as ordinary, nothing special, to the human children involved, is proof yet again as we have been taught to believe, that children (therefore all of us at some time), are born with this 'spirituality' – a natural awareness of spirit, which we so often lose growing up as we do in a material world. An incident that was natural, and therefore acceptable to the children, was processed as something 'paranormal', extraordinary, in the minds of the parents. According to Geoff, one of the fathers involved, he still goes cold, and the hairs on his arms still stand up, when he thinks about it.

(As an afterthought, it is interesting to note that the playroom was situated in the new part of the house and therefore, apparently, the children were witnessing the appearance of real spirit children and not a 'replay of a memory' or an 'image from the past', as in 'ghost', which might have been the case had it taken place in the old part.)

• • •

The experience of the children happened within the last few years and although the next vivid encounter with the spirit world took place a long time ago, its relevance in bringing hope and comfort to the recipient is timeless, and the theme of most of the encounters here recorded. Here is Jane's story.

> You might be interested in an experience I had some years ago when I was in hospital. I cannot call it a religious experience though it gave me an assurance of survival after death. It certainly was an unusual experience.
>
> I have worked on medical research problems all my life until I retired a few years ago.

In my mid-twenties I was in hospital with a severe injury to my spine and unable to walk. I was working as a lecturer. I was also engaged to be married.

After being a week or two in hospital and not improving, I was feeling very depressed. One evening the sister came in and tried to cheer me up by saying they were going to pray for me in chapel that evening and I must not lose heart –there was always Lourdes. That night I was lying awake when my bedroom door was pushed open and a colleague came in from the school, an elderly man, named S, from the same department in which I worked. He was a brilliant scholar and a good friend of mine. He sat by my bed holding my hands, talking cheerfully and telling me to keep up my courage, for I was going to get well and would be back again at my work. He seemed to stay with me a long time and he looked just as he always did, in a black alpaca coat and very short hair, iron grey. I only realised he had gone when the night sister looked in. She said I looked better.

I told her I had had such a nice visitor, who had cheered me wonderfully. She laughed at me and said, 'We don't allow visitors at this time of night. Do you know it is two o'clock?' This did not worry me. I knew he had come in somehow.

The next day my chief (the professor from the school) came to see me with the good news that a new expert on spinal troubles was coming to see me that afternoon. I thanked him and said I was feeling full of hope, as old S had been to see me last night and had restored some of my courage. I saw his face change.

He rubbed the back of his head, a habit when he was worried, and said, 'I am sorry about this. We did not tell you, as we thought it would upset you, but old S died a fortnight ago.'

I did recover after about four months and returned to my job.[1]

• • •

A driver with the NHS, picking up patients and taking them to the hospital for treatment, stopped to pick up an elderly lady. She got on the bus but when he came to drop her off she wasn't there. On questioning the other passengers, nobody else had seen her, but the driver knew that he had!

When people have a paranormal experience, they know they have had one. Experiences, it seems, can come into our lives in a variety, a multitude of ways, the following incident involving a spiritual healer a very simple, ordinary example of 'thought', or 'strong impression' making some sort of connection.

Jean Pace was giving healing to an elderly gentleman when she felt a strong impulse to give him, symbolically, a red rose from the other side of life. She tried to push this impulse to one side as she didn't believe in giving clairvoyant 'messages' while healing. At the end of the healing session, there it was with her again, and she argued with herself, 'What do I want to be giving an elderly gentleman a red rose for?' and felt he would just laugh at her. As he was leaving, she did tell him, however, and imagine her surprise when he told her it was his wedding anniversary that day.

• • •

In seeking to separate truth from imagination, fact from fiction, we must pause and ask ourselves, 'Is there a natural explanation for the seemingly strange things that happen?' We must weigh up all the facts, all the evidence, before convincing ourselves something 'out of the ordinary' has occurred. As many of us are aware, there is a never-ending play of forces, influences, energies, surrounding us, awake or asleep, and it could be a temptation to assume that something with a natural explanation is 'something else'. A highly intelligent, essentially practical gentleman recently made the comment, 'There is a lot more out there than we realise.' But we must be on guard against being too gullible, too easily convinced, looking closely at the incident, and scrutinising, analysing, challenging in the search for a natural explanation rather than a supernatural one. The balance, it seems, is an extremely fine one, as in the case of the healer who felt strongly persuaded to tell the elderly gentleman about the rose. She doubted her own impression yet finally, possibly because she was 'nagged' into giving it – apparently this can be one way we assess if a thought is genuine, if it persists – she had to tell him, and it seems she was right to do so. Seemingly 'thoughts', 'impressions', if strong, can be a way in which we receive 'tuition'; help, guidance, through 'intuition'.

Janice was seriously ill after a routine operation – it turned out she was haemorrhaging and was rushed to the medical ward and put on a drip. That night, as she slipped in and out of consciousness, she remembers hearing a male voice softly telling her to 'sit up', saying she had fluid on her lungs and to 'sit up and it will clear'. She described it: 'With the voice came an angelic presence radiating pure love towards me, filling me with calm.' Listening to the advice, despite the struggle and the pain, she forced herself to sit upright in her bed. The visitor returned again the next night bringing others with him, and although she couldn't see them, she could feel them all around her, and again the room was filled with peace. She also had an overwhelming feeling that she was going to be 'OK'.

A week later, Janice was stable enough to go home, but a return visit to the hospital proved to her the reality of her angelic visitors. The doctors discovered a blood clot on her lungs and, 'Sitting up in bed, just like the spirit said, saved my life.' The doctors informed Janice that if she had been lying down, she could have drowned in her own blood.[2]

• • •

An artificial flower, found in a peculiar position, had a positive and clear message for a couple when they didn't know what to do.

It was the early eighties, Runcorn, Cheshire. Alice and Harry Owen's only daughter had now left home, and they thought about moving into a bungalow in the same area. But they weren't sure. Undecided as to what to do, they casually looked around until one day, turning up to view yet another property, they had the answer. As they stepped into the hallway of the empty bungalow there, lying in the middle of the floor, impossible to ignore, was a flower – an iris. The significance of this was not lost on Alice and Harry. There and then they agreed to the purchase of the bungalow, where they lived for many happy years. And the reason why the flower was instrumental in the decision-making? Iris, the name of the flower, is also the name of their daughter.

• • •

It seems to be that if a person is meant to 'see' something, perhaps a 'light' or some form of 'apparition', they are usually attracted to look towards where it will happen. They are drawn by a noise, a movement, by something that makes them 'aware'; in other words they are prepared for the experience, otherwise apparently, it would be a wasted effort on the part of the 'other side', so quick is the vibration. Again, as in the case of the artificial flower, noticing the striking position ordinary objects are found in when they are meant to be noticed, can we consider the intriguing story of the blue plastic bottle top?

Three close friends worked together in the clothing department of a large supermarket in the north of England. One of them, Tracey, a mother of two, in her late thirties, was diagnosed with a brain tumour on New Year's Eve, 2003. She passed away in March 2004.

Gill, her closest friend, and a number of others from the supermarket, sat together in church waiting for the funeral service to begin. One of the girls thought she had better slip out to the toilet before the service began, and quietly eased her way out of the pew. As she stepped into the aisle, she was surprised to see a blue plastic bottle top lying there. The others noticed it and they were all struck by the odd look it had, a plastic bottle top sitting in such a prominent place, in a church. They puzzled about it, questioning how it could have got there.

The next day, at work as usual, Gill was in the storeroom and left a small plastic water bottle empty, but with the top on, ready to be re-filled at lunch time. It was a while later when, returning to pick it up, she cried out in shock as she saw written inside, down the length of the bottle, the name Tracey. Frantically she called the others into the room and showed them the bottle, not saying what she had seen, just shouting, 'Look.' They all saw it. Clearly written, on the inside of the bottle, where there could have been no intervention, and in what seemed to be a child's handwriting with a capital T and R, formed out of the condensation in the bottle, was the name Tracey. The name of the friend whose funeral they had attended only the day before. Sobered, they held the bottle up against some dark clothing in the storeroom where they were able to view it even more clearly. And as they looked, as if having made its statement, satisfied that they had registered the phenomena, it gradually evaporated, and was no more.

• • •

Strange, unexplainable things that happen; things that give cause for thought. Diane Woolridge soon knew the answer to the dime that kept turning up in the most unusual places.

Diane, a Canadian, lives in Winnipeg. She is in her early fifties and has three grown-up sons living away from home. Her husband Joe, who passed away in the summer of 2003, was a welder. He had his own small welding business and she was his book-keeper. Diane tells how she had always been careful with money. 'Penny pinching', her husband called it. He would say to her, 'Just buy what you want, don't worry about the money, you've got plenty, enjoy it.' But she could never get rid of that feeling to 'count the pennies'; (a dime is equivalent to what we would call a penny). She was so devastated by his passing that she recalls going through every emotion. Anger that he had left her, sadness, hurt; and she tried to describe how she could not pray; she could not turn to God. Instead she kept asking the question over and over again in her mind, 'Why did this have to happen to him?' But she says she has definitely felt his presence, and told me the story about the dime.

Not long after his passing, Diane would unexpectedly find a dime, in various places, sometimes just lying in the road. She would laugh as she picked it up, remembering his words about her 'penny pinching'. Then, finding a dime happening so often, she slowly began to realise it was more than coincidence. At first she continued to laugh when it happened, and if anyone was with her and asked what she was laughing at, she would just shrug it off as nothing, not saying what she was starting to believe. That it was her husband's way of communicating with her. When finding a dime started to happen in unusual, remarkable ways, she knew for certain that he was there, and she felt able to face life again.

She found a dime one day in the middle of the kitchen floor.

There was no one else at home at the time and no explanation for how it had got there. And she thought how strange it was, seeing it lying right in the middle of the floor (again as in the other stories, attracting attention). Another time she opened the front door and there was a dime lying on her doorstep. No one had been to the house, and there was no possible explanation for it other than that it was from her husband. She started thinking of the old song, 'Pennies from Heaven', and every time it happened, she accepted it as such. Diane belongs to the local bowling team, and after a game, they go to a pub, have a drink, and play pool. One night the barman directed them to a certain pool table and when Diane walked across and stood in front of it, there, perched on the edge, was a dime.

• • •

But are we too gullible? Do we read something special into incidents that are merely coincidence, just 'one of those things'? In a deeply emotional state, it is often easy to make a mountain out of a molehill as the saying goes. However, and whatever our state of mind, as has already been remarked on, the fact remains that when people have a paranormal experience, they know they have had one, and no one will convince them otherwise.

Linda Johnson, a nurse from Crieff in Scotland, gave birth to her baby at 5.30 a.m. At the same time, her mother, who lived fifty miles away and who did not know what was happening, got out of bed and for no apparent reason started wandering round and round, worried and restless. Suddenly she knew that the baby had been born, and later marvelled at the 'power', 'presence', that had awakened her and linked her into the event. Perhaps a trivial paranormal experience to the non-participant, but to the recipient, a never-to-be-forgotten one, and one that proved to her that there is indeed 'something there'.

Incidents, strange incidents, often born out of the ordinary, happen in life all the time, noticed, perhaps remarked on, and then forgotten until brought to mind by some conversation. Everyone has a tale to tell of the so-called paranormal. If it is not a story that they themselves have experienced, then they have a story that has been told to them, and the conversation usually carries on with, 'Well I don't personally believe in anything like that but something happened'...and on it goes. A very 'unbelieving' archaeologist recently told me – with a nervous laugh – 'I'm a real sceptic about such things but there was one incident.' He told how he had been working with a team of archaeologists on a site five to six thousand years old and they couldn't find certain drains and trenches. Finally someone suggested bringing in the dowsers – experts who search for water and underground minerals using forked sticks. The dowsers immediately led them to what they had been looking for, leaving my archaeologist friend amazed and deciding to be more 'open-minded' in future.

Ordinary, everyday experiences can herald a great turning point in our lives. (A seemingly ordinary event in an ordinary life has often been the inspiration for inventions that have affected centuries of lives – think of Isaac Newton and his apple; and it is often through an ordinary event that the greatest discoveries have been made. Historians and scientists discussing a Second World War project on BBC 2 agreed that 'the simplest ideas are always the best'.) And so it seems that in the miraculous touching of our lives, the 'unnamed something', the 'universal energy', the 'life force', 'God', often reaches out through the mundane, the trivial, the ordinary, charging it with that 'special something', imbuing it with greater meaning, significance; telling us 'we are never alone'.

• • •

The last few years have seen a change in the way that people treat paranormal experiences. Whereas at one time it was taboo to talk about such things (normal people would not be associated with such talk), for many reasons, including the revolution of the Internet, stories and experiences and literature are accessible to people all over the world, and we are now opening up and sharing stories freely.

Stan Walker was badly affected by the death of his sister Jean. He had always been close to Jean, and perhaps the biggest hurt was the fact that she seemed to have gone without there being any sense of closeness between them, or any sign to him of what was about to happen. Stan found it difficult to explain, but when other members of their large family had passed, he had the feeling or sense that something was still there. Being close to his sister, he had expected a similar feeling.

Not long after the funeral, he went alone to visit the grave, and stood talking to her, trying to express his feelings and asking her for a sign that she was still close. Sadly he made his way home. He walked along a path in the cemetery that led him to a gap in the hedge, a popular short cut. As he made to pass through the gap, Stan noticed, on a branch sticking out in front of him, a card that had obviously blown away from the flowers on a grave. On the card was his sister's name.

It must have been coincidence. Perhaps that's the most popular expression used when trying to explain away something out of the ordinary that has happened; but it is not always so. Margaret Brady lives in Ohio. Her husband died suddenly, and since then, she says he flashes the lights in her home now and again. He was in charge of the town supply of electricity! After her husband Raymond died, Dorothy's telephones played 'radio'! At the start of his engineering career, Raymond worked in radio. A young girl never forgot her auntie phoning to tell her that her mother had died. The girl already knew, but how did her auntie know? She couldn't have known either that or other information she relayed to her, through the usual systems.

. . .

Coincidence, but what does the word mean? The dictionary classifies coincidence as:

A notable concurrence of events or circumstances without apparent causal connection.

There is another definition of a coincidence, a very old saying, not found in dictionaries or academic studies but believed by many to be true.

A coincidence is God's way of performing a miracle anonymously.

And we can perhaps know that something is more than coincidence when we take into consideration the all-round picture, the circumstances, the emotions involved, and the 'need'. The following incident, Peter's story (which some might call coincidence), though short and precise, has the hallmark of the other side of life in its endeavour to reach us in sad, difficult times.

Peter, always a fit, happy man – having just retired at the age of fifty-five and with his wife looking forward to a full, comfortable future – tragically found himself to be terminally ill. After almost two years of illness and nearing the end of his life, yet still able to go out, he started the engine of his car and as he did so was drawn to notice the mileage on the clock. He was amazed to see that the numbers were those of his mother's Co-op dividend number, well known to him when a boy, running the errands. At a time when he badly needed her, suddenly seeing this number (the fact that he even noticed it in itself was remarkable) suggested to him that, from the other side of life, his mother had made her presence known. Reaching out to someone in need is the essence of contact from the other side, and if that contact is made through numbers, then so be it. It is the message that is important, not the method.

But the tale of Steven Smith and the numbers is a difficult one to understand. Steven, a practical man in his mid-forties, runs a successful security business with his brother. For some years he has had strange things happening in his life but has been able to account for them as being either warnings, or simply perhaps (to quote his casual way of accepting paranormal experiences) proof that there **is** more to life than we realise. However, this is not the case with the numbers. He is haunted by the way that certain numbers repeatedly turn up in his life in a variety of situations; and while the numbers themselves often have a meaning, as yet he has found no meaning for why they happen.

The number 9 – 11 is prominent with Steven, it crops up almost every day in an ordinary sort of way but the way it happened while he was on holiday was especially remarkable. He travelled with his partner to Malaysia, twenty-five hours' flying time. Exhausted after the gruelling flight, they were met at the airport by a transit van to take them to their hotel. On stepping into the van, Steven noticed the time on the dash-board clock. It was 9 – 11.

Back home again, he was out in the early hours of the morning on a long distance call for work. On the way home (it was 3.00 am) a vehicle passed him with the registration number V.911.

The table number while he was on holiday was 38, his father's police number. (His father died soon after retiring from the force.) Some time ago he bought a plot of land, it was number 37. The plot number usually stays as the house number when it is built but the builders, for one reason or another on completion, changed his house number to 38.

His grandfather's police number, 11, also turns up regularly in his life and it too was the number of a house he once lived in.

These numbers, 'sharing' his life, occur regularly enough and in experiences strong enough to make him take notice and wonder why.

• • •

It is thought that there are different meanings for different numbers, and that every number has an importance, a vibration of its own. Numbers and names supposedly help to carry us through this lifetime and the lessons we learn. Here is Elizabeth's story, where we find a link between the number 666 and a vivid dream (a vision as she calls it) of steps.

Elizabeth Lillico, an attractive blonde in her early thirties, lives near Newcastle on Tyne. She has had employment ranging from eight years in a casino to her present post, an assistant in a Mind, Body and Spirit shop. It appears that her present position, and her interest in all related topics, has helped her to understand strange things that happen in her life. For example, over a year ago she had a frightening dream (vision) of being taken up a huge flight of free-standing steps (steps without a rail or sides, which she is afraid of anyway). She was so afraid of the steps in her dream that she pulled away from the person trying to persuade her to walk up them and ran away. The dream disturbed her but she could find no explanation for it, until months later.

Because of another series of events she decided, unexpectedly, to have a holiday in Egypt, a place that holds a fascination for her. Immediately on booking the holiday, the number 666 appeared on the shop till roll as she served a customer, and having worked in a casino – it appears that 666 is important in the roulette layout numbers – numbers do have a meaning for her. She wondered if the 666 was a warning to her not to go to Egypt, but, whatever it was, she knew it had a meaning. Idly watching a sports programme on television one day, not really interested, she suddenly felt drawn to notice the number on the back of a shirt worn by a foreign footballer, it was 666.

Months later, driving down the motorway to Manchester Airport for her holiday, she again spotted the number 666.

Elizabeth loved Egypt; she felt it was her spiritual home, and early on in the holiday she attempted to walk up a flight of steps without rails or sides, in other words, free standing. A man tried to encourage her to go to the top, saying there was the most beautiful view, but fear took over, and she ran away from him, upset. Elizabeth later realised that they were the same steps she had seen in her dream months earlier, long before she had even thought about going to Egypt. She was amazed at the dream and the reality being as one.

Towards the end of the holiday, Elizabeth did manage to conquer her fear and walk to the top of similar steps with a group of people. Overcome by the beauty of the vista stretched out in front of her, and pleased that she had met the 'challenge of the steps', she also knew that the holiday was to have an important meaning in her life – partly because of a man she met up with and has continued to be in contact with. Elizabeth has also discovered that for her the number 666 could mean a warning, or a fear (possibly a fear of the steps which she did conquer), or a fear of moving on into the future.

• • •

Something ordinary happening, on an ordinary day, but then there are also extraordinary things...that happen.

When Bangau Samuel realised he was the only survivor of a plane crash in the Borneo jungle he put his faith in God. By the time he stumbled into the village of Pak Padi six days later, he had come to believe that he had been led to safety and fed by the ghost of his father, Juni Samuel, who was killed in the accident.

Bangau was among ten passengers and crew on a Britten-Norman Islander aircraft that crashed in bad weather (in 2002) in the dense Kayan forest in the Indonesian part of the island.

After peering into the cabin, he sensed his father's presence and heard a voice say, 'Get away from the plane and walk to the creek.'

Bangau walked and at night sheltered in a cave where he says he saw his father in a vision. The vision told him to buy some meatball soup, a local delicacy. 'It was as if I saw a street seller and just asked for food,' he said. He awoke the next day feeling as if he had eaten. On the fifth day he had a dream in which his father said, 'I have died but you are alive, so follow the creek until you find a village. Tell people there that you are my son and they will help you. Remember, you must stay alive and look after your mother.'

From then on Bangau kept walking. Early on the morning of the sixth day he met a local farmer who took him to his village and fed him. 'Doctors say Bangau is in fair condition but will be flown to Jakarta, the Indonesian capital, to be treated for pains in his chest and head.'[3]

• • •

The following story, which took place in South Africa in 1972, ranges from the miraculous to the extraordinary in a tale of astral travelling, or should we say an out-of-body experience, or does it encompass both?

Here is Mary Wilton's story.

> We lived in Johannesburg, South Africa, from 1970 to 1973 and it was there that the following incidents happened.
>
> My husband and I used to sit meditating for one hour a week. Not any special meditation, but really just a time of quiet contemplation and prayer, and maybe to develop any spiritual or psychic gifts we might have. During one session I saw paper money flying all over

the room, and the vision quickly changed into seeing my husband sitting swathed in bandages from top to toe. I didn't feel unduly concerned about this, not a worrying feeling at all, I just felt that he would be 'looked after', whatever that would mean.

Not a long time after that, he secured a very good contract which, on completion, would mean a lot of money for us. He was a builder and the contract was to do work on a block of flats which was being built. It was his first day and he was on the seventh floor balcony, eighty feet up. He stepped back, lost his footing, and fell, through scaffolding, into the ditch below. Miraculously, he got up and started to walk away. One of his men, who had been working at ground level, picked up his glasses which had shot off during the impact of the fall, and handed them to him saying, 'Here, boss.'

The site foreman and other workers who were in the site cabin at the time, saw him fall, and stunned, froze on the spot. No one wanted to go and see what was left of his body lying in the ditch. They were even more stunned when his head appeared over the side as, scrambling up, he made his way towards them. After countless x-rays, at two hospitals, he was found to have only one small rib bone broken in his back.

I arrived at the site a few hours later to collect his car. The site foreman met me. He was obviously still in a state of shock as he told me that, although they did not believe in such things, himself and the other workmen who had witnessed the accident had come to the same conclusion. Sincerely and simply he said, 'Your husband was caught and held by invisible arms.'

Much later that day (early evening), I finally talked to the consultant who had been brought over from Pretoria. He told me that had there not been as many witnesses to the fall (people waiting at a bus stop outside had also seen it happen and ran onto the site), no one would have believed it possible that a man could fall eighty feet – through scaffolding which should have broken every bone in his body on the way down – then get up and walk away. The consultant also told me that he should have been killed by the impact of the fall alone, from fatal internal injuries...

Shocked – I had kept myself together all day – and hardly able to believe that he was not seriously injured, after my talk with the consultant and in the privacy of our own home, I gave way to strong emotions. I cried and begged and prayed for help and finally, perhaps as a way of giving vent to feelings, wrote a short airmail letter to my close friend Jean, who lived in London, telling her of the accident and the miracle.

A few days later I received a letter from Jean. It was a short note really, asking if we were safe and well. She explained that she had been reading in bed, late at night, when she was drawn to look at the foot of the bed. 'And there you were, standing,' she wrote, 'in a very distressed state.' This must have happened at the same time as my trauma, my distressed state. Our letters had crossed in the post. There was no way Jean could have known about the accident.

• • •

There are endless extraordinary stories, incidents, happenings, in daily life that are not necessarily easy to understand; or perhaps we are not meant to understand them at that particular point. But then, to pursue the argument, if we are not meant to understand them, why do they happen? (I don't suppose those are the sort of things a priest was meaning when he talked recently about 'the mysteries of life'.) But it does seem to be that there is a 'working out behind the scenes', a weaving and interweaving, so to speak, a preparation for what is about to happen. We could liken it to a play where there is often as much going on behind the scenes as out front. Kathleen Walker sensed something was different; bits and pieces, thoughts, feelings, incidents, all not adding up to anything, until later, when they began to make sense; but here is Kathleen's story.

It was 1986, and Kathleen was living in Hamilton, three miles south of Glasgow, with John her husband, who was forty-six years old, and son Stewart, twenty-one years old. Kathleen made a marvellous and quick recovery from a hysterectomy operation. She was out and about so quickly it was commented on, but it was only later, after the tragedy, that an elderly lady said to her, 'That's why you made such a rapid recovery, God knew what you had to bear.' It is thought-provoking that leading up to the tragedy her husband John seemed to talk about his family more than he had ever done. He mentioned especially his mother, who had died when he was two years old, and dwelt on reminiscences. Kathleen remembers feeling that she must be sure to have his sister's phone number and address in her diary, never having thought like that before in all their years of marriage, because John had the information.

They booked a holiday to Tenerife. Although at the time money was tight, they decided to make the effort and travel club class on the plane so that John could go in the cockpit during the flight and talk to the captain (his hobby was making and flying model planes). Not long before the holiday the airline wrote asking if they would accept a refund and travel ordinary class, as club class had been overbooked. Although the cheaper fare would have been welcome at the time, they decided 'no', they would stick with club class for John's sake, as they might never get another chance. The holiday and the flight were a big success.

Not long before the tragic event, a Saturday, the family went out shopping (with Kathleen's cousin Virginia and her family who were visiting them for the weekend). They were in Woolworth's playing around on a machine where you put a finger in and it gives a health statement. One after the other they tried the machine, Virginia giving a running commentary on each statement. When it came to John's turn, she said, 'And as for you John, you should be dead with a reading like that.'

A few weeks later, John, never ill, arrived at the sports centre as usual for his game of squash. He collapsed and died during the game.

• • •

Jan Wheatley is obviously someone who is 'in tune' with the other side, and through her vision, or understanding, is clearly able to pick up on any phenomenon relayed to her. Hers is another extraordinary tale and here she tells it, in her own words:

> Travelling home, late one Saturday evening, along the motorway, I heard an ambulance siren behind me (very loud). I automatically pulled over and looked through the mirror only to establish there was no ambulance. I immediately looked to my right, expecting to see it passing but once again no ambulance. Very surprised at this occurrence, I

continued my journey home and came to the conclusion that I had been given a warning.

On returning home I went straight to bed and that night my father came into my sleep state. I know we talked quite a lot but the only thing I can remember of any conversation was that as he walked away, he said, with a half smile on his face, 'They'll be all right.' When I woke up I told my husband that something was going to happen to the family but I didn't know what.

The next day was Sunday morning and it was approximately lunchtime. My youngest son's fiancé phoned me and asked if I would go straight away because my son was screaming with pain in his head. I did go and called a doctor immediately. He was rushed to hospital by ambulance (sirens blasting) and was diagnosed eventually with meningococcal septicaemia. I can remember looking at him in his bed being injected with morphine and I was thinking, 'I hope you're right, Dad.' Fortunately he was and my son survived.

A week later my mother was taken into hospital for major bowel surgery at sixty-nine. She came through her operation successfully but the week after she returned home she took a deep vein thrombosis and a pulmonary embolism and was taken back into hospital. Once again we were very worried, but fortunately, she survived and once again my father was right. When I recalled the sleep state experience he had actually said, **'They'll** be all right.'

Perhaps experiences are there to give us awareness, even if

we don't always register their significance at the time; perhaps, while a comfort to those who believe, they are a challenge to those who don't – a challenge to believe or find answers! A young vicar, well known, on television recently, told of his conversion to the church. He spoke of it as an amazing, sudden calling, during a service. During this particular service he recalled suddenly having this moment when he was praying, aware of God's presence around him; and he said to the presenter, it was 'more real even than the conversation I am having with you now'. His life changed from then on. What he really wanted to do, he continued, was to convince ordinary people to believe in something more than they can see with their own eyes.

What might go a little way to understanding why certain things happen is the old story of being shipwrecked on a desert island. One of the first things a survivor would want to do would be to reassure the people back home that he or she was safe. And so it is, as evidenced with those who die, pass on, go to the 'other side'. They are desperate to let us know they have survived so-called 'death', and in this desperation will try any means possible to attract our attention, make us take notice, be aware of their presence. And it is well recorded (by experts in this field), that our lack of understanding, or disbelief in life after death, or our refusal to be open-minded on the subject, is the biggest barrier to our discernment.

But then, there are those who have a natural awareness of the 'other side'. Nothing phases them about it and they relate stories and experiences as if they were talking about a day at the seaside. Such a lady was overheard in a café recently quite casually discussing the clocks in her house (reputedly a favourite trick of those passed over in their efforts to attract attention) which were forever being changed. Just as casually, she mentioned to her equally blasé companion that she had seen her deceased husband standing at the bottom of her bed. Apparently her immediate reaction on seeing him was to say, 'Go away, go away, I'm not ready to come yet.' How marvellous to react as naturally as that lady to what are thought of by many to be unnatural or paranormal happenings.

And yet, are such things so unnatural to the majority of people, or should we assume that it is a question of understanding. As mentioned earlier, it seems that most people, when talking about paranormal experiences, have either had one for themselves or can relate a story they have heard from someone else. Since starting this work it has been revealing to me the number of stories, experiences, tiny incidents there are 'out there' begging to be heard. Happenings that have caught people's attention have made them think, but all too often with no one to relate their thoughts to.

Recently, someone talking about her close friend Anne, relayed how Anne had been greatly uplifted by a chance encounter with a lady at her place of work. After hearing the story, I wondered, 'Was it a chance encounter?' Her friend works in a soft play facility. She had been struggling to come to terms with the death of her mother, three months previously. A complete stranger walked into the facility with her grandchildren and on seeing them settled and happily playing, walked over to have a chat with Anne. The routine conversation soon turned to – something else – and Anne was astounded to hear the lady telling her all sorts of things about her mother and personal details she could never have known. During the conversation, she would walk away for a few minutes, then return, as if remembering something else she had to say; all of it accurate. Finally, she said that Anne and her sister had each taken a flower from a wreath on the grave of their mother, as a keepsake. 'Yes, we did.' She then named the flower, and she was correct. The lady left and was never seen there again – she had never been seen there before, either.

That people need to have experiences of their own for proof is probably true and that they have them is probably true, but how aware are they? How many of us are aware that experiences, guidance, support, often take the form of 'thought'. Thoughts, we are told, are living things and thoughts (impressions, a sixth sense or intuition) may be the more usual way of receiving communication 'from beyond' when we need that special something. For it seems it is not only seeing that is involved in communication but being sensitive to the whole range of our emotions: feelings, premonitions, elation, déja vu – suspense, concern, excitement, smell, touch; having a sense of something and so on.

Viv Halliday is a woman who at times in her life has strong impressions about things, and is often amazed at their accuracy. None more so than, when newly married, she moved from the North of England to Cambridgeshire to be with her husband Doug, who was serving in the RAF.

When Viv and Doug moved to Chatteris, Cambridgeshire, they were given a flat that was isolated and miles away from the RAF camp. They expected to be there for three and a half years. Viv says she will never forget the feeling she had as she stepped into the flat for the first time. Although expecting to stay for a few years at least, she knew by the strong impression she had that they would not be there for long. It was only five weeks later when Viv became ill. Because of her illness, they were forced to move somewhere nearer to the camp.

Again, they were living in a flat at St Ives, Cambridgeshire, and expected to stay there for three and a half years. After only six months Viv had the same sort of feeling, the impression that they would be moving. Someone said that it would be nice for her mother to visit, have a holiday, and Viv, who would have liked nothing better than to have her mother stay with her said, 'She won't ever come here.'

One Sunday, out of the blue, she had the strong urge to start packing – to put away in boxes all the little ornaments and treasures they had collected over the years. Her husband watched her in amazement, collecting things, then packing them away. Failing to convince her that she was wrong in her feeling or impression that they would be moving, Doug thought, 'Well if you can't beat them, join them,' and he too started packing. Together they packed over three chests.

The next day, Monday, Doug was called to the office and told he had another posting. They had to be ready to leave the flat on the following Saturday. Luckily, because of Viv's strong impression, they had already filled over three chests out of the nine needed, so they comfortably packed the rest in good time for the move.

• • •

Gillian Prior, from Bedlington, Northumberland, was having difficulty with her daughter Rachel who was aged ten. There was no doubt that the child was ill with something but as she wouldn't say what was wrong with her, even the doctor couldn't get to the bottom of it. The girl would not say what was wrong, the school didn't seem to go too thoroughly into the problem, counsellors tried but even they couldn't sort it out. Gillian, puzzled and worried sick about the situation, didn't know where to turn. Could it be that one of the reasons for the child's illness was because a favourite aunt she was close to had died? Then she had moved to another school. The girl was in a group of friends and although everything seemed to be fair and above board, she often wondered about that situation too.

The worry continued for almost two years. One night, with the situation almost out of control and Gillian at her wit's end about it, she made, in her words, a 'heartfelt cry, a prayer of desperation for help'. 'The next morning', she said, 'as soon as

I put my foot out of bed I knew it would be OK and I knew what I had to do.' She called at the school with her daughter and talked to a girl who was supposed to be a friend but whom she knew left her alone at times. Following on from this conversation, she realised that it was, after all, what she had suspected, a case of bullying. She sent a message to another girl who was in the group and who, she discovered, was mainly responsible for the bullying, saying that it had to stop, that day. Gillian also saw the mother of this girl. No bullying ever happened again.

• • •

It was 1975 and a lady travelling from Amman airport had secured a comfortable window seat for her onward flight from Iran to England. She willingly surrendered this, however, to a sick boy with a painful leg condition. His father, a Jordanian Muslim, told her his son was going to London for specialist treatment for suspected carcinoma – his fate in God's hands. Shocked at this pious attitude, she confessed she didn't believe in God. He then tried to convince her of Allah's existence, telling her this was the twenty-sixth anniversary of something important to her. Recalling that it was her son's twenty-sixth birthday, she asked him how he knew. He replied that he had prayed for Allah's help in convincing her.[4]

• • •

Happenings, experiences, ordinary (but imbued with that 'something special'), or extra ordinary, what are they? Do they play perhaps the most important part in life, or are they merely the décor, the adornment, the colour that spices things up from time to time. Is it some divine intervention that has held and uplifted?

with the situation almost out of control, I made a heart-
felt cry, a prayer of desperation for help

Or is it all simply coincidence, a parody of what we would like
to believe is divine, is God? William James, in his book *The Varieties
of Religious Experience* explains: 'The essence of religious
experiences, the things by which we finally must judge them,
must be that element or quality in them which we can meet
nowhere else.' He continues, telling us that 'such a quality will
be most prominent and easy to notice in those religious
experiences which are most one-sided, exaggerated, and intense.'

Happenings, experiences that can, collectively or individually,
aid us, inspire us and conceivably set us on the challenge, the
adventure of a lifetime; happenings, experiences, that will
hopefully lead to our acceptance of the possibility, even the
certainty, of life afterlife.

• • •

A bouncy church was in the news recently. It is an inflatable church
that can go anywhere, with pulpit, pews, organ, stained glass
windows, but with a solid floor. A member of the public was
interviewed, and talking about the church when it was on display
commented, 'I think it will take more than that to bring people
back to the church – what we need to see is just the church being
relevant.'

According to recent statistics on an *Everyman* programme on
BBC2, only seven per cent of people attend church; many people
are uncomfortable with the name 'God' preferring to say 'energy'.
Over one third of Britons say they have had a sense or feel the
presence of someone who has passed away, and fifty-five per cent
believe in an afterlife. While today the interest in mediums is at
an all-time high.

To recall the words of the young vicar mentioned earlier in

the chapter, when he said that all he wanted to do is to convince ordinary people 'to believe in something more than they can see with their own eyes', is perhaps not such a difficult task after all!.

Chapter Two

'How slight the shadow that is holding us apart'[1]

IN THIS NEW MILLENNIUM, it is as if we have had to wait the passing of a full cycle of time for the wheel of life to halt its spinning on 'truth'. It seems to be that man is once again waking up to the fact that he is not merely a physical being, and that, to realise his full potential, he must be aware that there are many more sides to existence than the material world would suggest.

One aspect of life in which we all partake is dreaming. We all dream. Whether we remember our dreams or not, they do happen, and the numbers of people who give credence to the dream state are growing. Stores are full of books on dreams. To quote one advert for such a book,

> Use dream analysis to reach new levels of self-awareness
> and learn valuable lessons about your life.

We are advised to sift out and to note what could be, if interpreted correctly, a message of vital importance to assist us in our waking.

> For dreams are that of which the subconscious is made;
> any condition is first dreamed before 'becoming reality'.[2]

Early man knew how to interpret his dreams, seeing them as revelations from God, from nature, from his ancestors; holding them as all-important in life and treating them with respect and awe. The Bible has many examples of extraordinary dreams or visions in which seers have been asked to interpret the meanings, for example the dreams of Pharaoh, interpreted by Joseph. But throughout history, dreaming has played a significant part in the lives of some of our greatest artists, writers, statesmen and scientists, as well as in the humdrum life of all 'ordinary' humans.

Margaret Smith tells us of her remarkable vision and its consequences, which happened in 1998.

> I had left my home to live with my mother, looking after her as she had started with Alzheimer's disease. My husband was working in the Middle East and our home was less than a mile away from my mother's. She died after six years but I stayed on, not having the heart to rush into 'selling' and moving back to my own home.

> A year and a half after her death, in 1998, the night before my husband was due home on a short, ten-day leave, I had a vision. In it, I was sitting on a double bed that was strewn with what I took to be legal papers. My dad, who had died sixteen years before, was sitting beside me, going through the papers and drawing my attention to them. My mother, looking exactly as I remembered her when I was a young girl, was standing behind us talking to a young man, completely ignoring my dad and I. Finally, wondering about this, I asked my dad if my mother was happy. His reply was so clear and emphatic that it startled me. 'She's unsettled,' he said, 'very unsettled,' and then I awoke.

The vision haunted me, and talking it over with my husband immediately we met at the airport the next morning, we both agreed that my mother was unsettled because she wanted me back in my own home. I had not felt able, emotionally, to make the final decision to sell my mother's house and move back into my own home, but within days of seeing the vision, I arranged for an estate agent to call and the house was valued. And although I had stressed to the agent that it was not to go on the market for at least another month (I just felt I needed more time to brace myself for the trauma of it all.), it was sold the next day within ten minutes of viewing. The agent had made a special request for one client to view.

In the event, I was saved the stress of having to show maybe dozens of people around, the main thing I was dreading. It was fortunate for me, as I needed to have everything settled, and be back in my own home, ready to face the sad and tragic events that followed less than two years later.

About ten years ago, Alexandra Connaught, a Mexican lady living in Cancun, in her twenties at the time, had a vivid dream. In the dream, her grandmother appeared to her strong and real saying, 'I want to give you a kiss.' Alexandra actually felt the kiss and was so surprised at this that the following morning she made the journey by bus to her grandmother's house. On arrival, the family told her that her grandmother had died, and they had been trying to contact her. Alexandra said that she felt 'good' about her grandmother's passing because in the dream, as she had seen her, her grandmother was happy, and had given her 'the kiss'. She believed that this was her grandmother's way of saying 'goodbye'.

. . .

The ancients talked of dreams as passing through two gateways, describing one as ivory, and the other horn. Apparently a dream that deludes us passes through the ivory gate; a true dream passes through the gate of horn. But, as we are informed, it is only when we ourselves begin to read or think through our dreams that we become aware of their significance. This awareness can lead us on to the thought, even provide the evidence, that our daily lives are not the only 'reality' and that in dreaming we are projected into another realm of life (reality) that is boundless. It is well known that some of the greatest inventions of mankind have been born out of the magic of 'day dreams', and there is overwhelming evidence to support this theory in literature, art and music.

Premonitions, which often occur in dreams foretelling the future (President Abraham Lincoln dreamed about his own assassination a week before he died), are a known fact, and often acted on; perhaps being warned not to travel on a certain flight or train, as in the case of Russell Grant, astrologer and medium. He dreamt he was looking at the clock on Euston station and the time was 4.10 but then the time suddenly changed to 7.25. Days later, one of his friends was due to go to Blackpool from Euston on the 4.10 train. Remembering his dream, Russell warned him to catch the next train. The 4.10 train was derailed and his friend could have been killed or injured. Instead he remembered Russell's advice and caught the next one, which was 7.25.

The psychiatrist Dr John Barker collected cases of premonitions after the 1966 mining disaster at Aberfan, Wales. Eryl Mai Jones who became a victim of the tragedy was nine years old at the time. Two weeks before, she had told her parents that she was not afraid to die because she would go to heaven with two of her friends whom she named. Before going to school on the morning of the disaster, she described having a dream of a black pile falling on the school, and then it disappeared. Eryl and her two friends died when the school was submerged.

History is full of so-called odd forebodings, strange feelings or warnings in dreams; but dreams can also be the heralders of good news.

Matilda Newton, who lived in Hunwick, c/o Durham, was distraught with worry. Wilfred, her son, forged his age and enlisted as a boy soldier in the 1914-18 war. He was at the front in the thick of the fighting and she hadn't heard from him for two years. Peace was declared but there was still no news of Wilfred. One night, in a dream, she saw him walking towards her. He was smiling and surrounded by light. Though dim at first, it gradually brightened as he drew closer to be seen finally standing on the front doorstep of their home. At this point in the dream Matilda suddenly woke up with a feeling of elation. She was convinced that the dream was an assurance of his safe return, but the family tried to discourage her from believing in what they thought was false hope. Only a few days later, in the early hours of the morning, loud banging on the front door caused her to rush downstairs where, on opening it, she found Wilfred standing on the doorstep, smiling, exactly as she had seen him in her dream.

• • •

Elderly people are often heard to say that the older they become, the more life seems to have been a dream. The language of dreams is universal. The language of the unconscious, the doorway to ESP (extra sensory perception); and there is also a thought that in the dream state we are gradually prepared for passing – as we become aware of the spirit world or 'going home' as it is often called. And yet, it is strange how, for whatever reason, meanings – and obvious ones at that – can sometimes be covered over, hidden from our understanding. Jean Bather, who, throughout her life, had studied many religions and understood ESP (healing, clairvoyance, dreams, visions), could not understand the meaning of a simple, all too clear (to others) dream. In the dream, her mother was talking to her and repeating the words, 'Come home, Jean, come home.' Jean told how she argued with her mother in the dream saying, 'But I *am* at home.' Some time later, Jean passed to the other side, seemingly still oblivious to the meaning of her dream.

There are endless tales of joyous reunion in the dream state, of meeting up with loved ones who have died, either in normal dreaming (when it does appear to the dreamer to be simply a dream, or lucid dreaming when the dreamer knows it as reality). Lucid dreams are often thought of as visions. A typical vision is one told by Norah. Norah Bowmaker was heartbroken by the passing of her husband Jack when she was in her sixties. She bravely carried on with life, never complaining, keeping the love they had shared deep in her heart. Years later she had a vision which she confided to her daughter-in-law. In it Norah told of finding herself in a beautiful garden and there, not far away, was Jack. He walked towards her, they met, then walked away hand in hand. Norah had no doubt that she had seen her husband in the garden and that for a brief moment they had been reunited. Such are the visions, the experiences, where we acknowledge the possibility of there being more to life than we can see with our own eyes; and these are the visions where we have perhaps, in a super conscious state, been privileged to catch a glimpse of life after life.

• • •

Normal dreaming, lucid dreaming, visions, astral travelling; what do they all mean? Scientists have endeavoured for years to encapsulate these altered states of consciousness and still the 'essence', the 'spark', the very nature of the experiences elude them. And, just as when a person has a paranormal experience, they *know* they have had one, so it is with all out-of-body experiences (referred to as OBEs) whether they are lucid dreams or near-death experiences (NDEs).

In February 2003 the BBC broadcast a programme *The Day I Died*, featuring what has been labelled as probably the most convincing documented case of a near-death experience to date. The lady concerned had major surgery to remove an aneurism in the wall of the large artery at the base of the brain. The doctor, in describing this daring operation, explained how the body temperature was lowered to 60°F, the heartbeat and breathing were stopped and the blood drained from the patient's head. She (the patient) described hearing the noise of the surgeon's saw as he opened her skull, and this noise seemed to be pulling her out of her body to where she had a clear view of everything that was going on. She described the instruments used – and these had been carefully concealed in boxes for reasons of hygiene – until needed in the actual operation. It was later stated that there was no way she could have seen what she described, which included several unusual things, or overheard the conversations she reported. All were confirmed.

In the interview she gave, following an amazing recovery, she told how she felt pulled through a tunnel at high speed towards a light where she heard her grandmother calling. She then saw an uncle who had passed away quite young and who had taught her to play the guitar. She saw other relatives and had an emotional reunion with her grandmother and uncle and wanted to stay with them. They reminded her that she had two young children to return to, but, pleading to stay, she explained that the children would be well loved and taken care of and all she wanted to do was to stay in this wonderful place, in the light...

Finally her uncle, insisting that she had to go back, accompanied her through the tunnel and then to the operating theatre where she described seeing her 'poor pitiful body'. Her uncle gave her a push and she remembers clearly 'diving' back into her body and feeling the pain. During the interview she also said that her life had been changed completely by the near-death experience, insisting that there is no such thing as death; 'death is nothing, nothing at all', and that the word 'dead' should be taken out of language as it is meaningless.

• • •

Richard Wilson's near-death experience, though not as dramatic as the one just recorded, was vivid enough and meaningful enough to have stayed with him as something 'special' that happened, throughout his life – he is now in his seventies.

It was in Yorkshire, early December 1950. After a serious operation Richard was aware that he was drifting in and out of consciousness all day. He remembers his mother at the end of the bed, and that he was distressed and in a state of shock, and that they raised his feet and took the drip off, as that was distressing him. Later that night, he remembers it being very quiet; he was in a side ward with dimmed lights when he came to, and there were a few people around the bed. He made a remark about the place being crowded and then he floated off again. Then, he remembers himself as being 'above the scene', not part of it. There were no lights or tunnels, just peace and calm; a feeling of being totally enclosed in 'nothing'. A lovely feeling. And he strongly remembers knowing that he was **not alone.**

Months later, after he got over the illness, a group scout leader remarked that he had changed.

• • •

A lady tells the story of how, in 1930, after the protracted, difficult birth of her daughter, she felt she was whirling in a long black tunnel with a bright, glowing opening at the end. She records how at last she reached the end of the tunnel where she floated gently in warm, soft, mist, in golden sunlight, with soft music and a feeling of complete happiness and the 'peace which passes understanding'. Faces smiled at her then faded away. She felt fully conscious and knew that she had died yet still lived. God's plan was good and death indeed had no sting. Then she remembered her baby and wondered who would look after her if she remained. She woke to the stinging pain of the doctor's hard slaps on both sides of her face. He said she'd given him the biggest shock of his life, to which she responded that it had been absolutely wonderful and he must not begrudge her the experience. Years later, she is still humbly grateful for what happened and has no fear of death, which she knows is as simple as walking from one room to another.[3]

It is well documented that one of the most impressive features of the near-death experience is the profound effect it has on the majority of those who experience it. They become more spiritual; often change careers and lifestyle so that they can be of service to others; they describe the experience as one of great beauty and love, and one person described it as their 'heart on fire with love' and purposefulness. Whatever happens has a meaning. Blind people have reported becoming sighted for the first time and there are those who tell of feeling as if they've 'come home'.

In a book published in London in 1697 there are nine cases of near-death experience, beginning with a case at Cologne in 1537, and including the well authenticated story of Anne Atherton.

Anne Atherton was fourteen years old when she fell sick with what the doctors described as an 'Anomalous Ague'. She lost her speech and fell into a death like trance that lasted for seven days, in November 1669. Those attending her detected more warmth 'than usually is in dead bodies', but having tried putting the looking glass to her mouth and later, burning coals to her feet, and she failed to respond, it was concluded that she was dead.

At her mother's request, the girl was not prepared for burial. After seven days, it was noticed that there was still warmth in her body.

Finally, after rubbing her with warm cloths, the girl revived, regained her speech, and called for her mother, recounting to her what had happened during her state of trance. She described being taken to heaven by an angel who showed her 'things glorious and unutterable, as Saints and Angels and all in glorious apparel'. She heard 'unparallel'd music divine; Anthems and Hallelujahs', but was told by the angel that she would not be allowed to enter heaven. She was told to go back again for a while and take leave of her friends and after a short time she would be admitted.

Anne did recover from her experience to live for four more years before finally departing, as recorded, 'with great assurance of her happiness hereafter'.

• • •

Out-of-body experiences (OBEs), or astral travelling, can occur during sleep or perhaps when sitting relaxed in a chair during the day. Records of such experiences are to be found in the literature of almost every age and nation. Some of the earliest experiences recorded are those of Socrates and Plotinus. Apparently they can just 'happen':

Mary Sadler's husband Jack was seriously ill in hospital, unable to communicate at all, but he appeared to her one night in their home standing by her bedside, wearing the clothes that he always wore, a fair isle pullover and a green and brown checked shirt. She was not asleep. Mary asked him what he was doing there, then, suddenly feeling afraid, looked away for a split second, then back, but he was gone.

He had not passed, but Mary knows that he visited her that night. She still cannot comprehend the fact that he came home, yet she saw him again later, so ill in hospital. It seems the difficulty of an out-of-body experience is often that of not knowing if it happened in our 'reality', or if it was 'something else'.

In an 'out-of-body' or 'astral travelling' experience, Iris Wilding from Northumberland got more than she bargained for, and the proof along with it, the next morning.

While asleep one night, Iris somehow left her body and transported herself to a zoo where a huge gorilla, on the loose, was rampaging among crowds of people. Terrified, the screaming crowds scattered hither and thither, desperate to keep out of the path of the raging animal. But Iris somehow felt safe, knowing he couldn't see her in her spirit body.

The next morning, she switched on the TV to see on a news programme, people running all over the place screaming, terrified. A gorilla had got loose in a zoo. In California.

June had a new romance. Eighteen months after her divorce it was strange to be dating again and a younger man at that. But they seemed made for each other right from the start, and life had suddenly become rosy and bright after the dark, hurtful months of the divorce.

One morning, on waking and reflecting on the previous night when she had been out with John (her new man friend), June had a strange feeling. She knew exactly where they had been, what had happened, what they had discussed – but there was 'something else'. Had they really been to this other place that was still so vivid in her mind, and had they really had this 'other' conversation? Confused and concerned, she talked it over with her father.

Over the years, her father and herself had proved the reality of astral travelling on at least two occasions. Now she wondered if it had happened again, but this time involving John. The main part of this 'other' conversation (if indeed that was what it was) being that John had told her he was waiting to appear in court as a witness, something to do with a tax enquiry in the firm where he worked. Her father advised her that the only way to sort it out was to ask John about it, but how could she ask him? She felt she didn't know him well enough to pose such a question, and anyway, he might think she was mad! They were in a pub when this supposed conversation took place and although she could describe precisely the setting – they were sitting in a booth with polished wood, high-backed chairs – she had no idea of the name of the pub or even where it was.

That night she was both curious and anxious when she met John. Not being able to erase the scene of the previous night from her mind, she knew that she had to sort it out, find out, one way or the other, if it had happened or not. They decided to go to the airport for an hour or two and view the coming and going of planes from the balcony. As they stood there, leaning casually on a handrail, June gradually brought the conversation round to the previous evening. She talked about the pub with the high-backed polished wood chairs. No real response from John except a sort of sideways look; then she blurted out the question, 'Did you say you are appearing in court...as a...?' His sudden, rapid movement, taking two or three strides away from her, unnerved her and she couldn't continue the question. He stood and stared at her, speechless for a moment, before finally saying, 'How did you know about that?' 'You told me.' 'Oh no I didn't, no one outside the firm knows about it yet.' Then, thoughtfully, and slowly, he made his way back to stand by her side.

• • •

In the following out-of-body experience the lady states specifically that she was seeing in colour, which is thought by some to be a sign of an experience with a spiritual source.

Three months after her mother's death, it was in 1961, while dozing on the couch (her dog was in the kitchen), she was suddenly aware of her body three feet above the couch, looking at herself in full colour, lying, eyes closed, with her dog stretched out beside her. Very troubled and trying not to return to her body, she became aware of her mother (a greyish-white figure) standing behind the couch and felt close to her in spirit. Her mother put a hand out to touch her head after which she awoke to find her dog not in the kitchen, but as she'd viewed it when out of her body.

Another time when this same lady was dreaming – again in bright pastel colours – she was floating away from the earth, and, as she thought of people she loved (her two dead sisters and her dead father), they were beside her and she felt pure happiness and peace. She can still recall the feeling, years later.[4]

When a case is not medically authenticated and there is therefore no way of knowing the seriousness of the condition, it is hard for anyone to assess if the person involved had an out-of-body experience or a near-death experience. But in another difficult birth, in the Midlands, Joan B. lost four pints of blood and was very ill in hospital. She suddenly found herself inside a tunnel with a pinprick of light at the end. She remembers falling to the sides of the tunnel, it was warm, but something kept pressing her to the light. She was arguing with herself that she wanted to stay in the tunnel where it was warm and not to go to the light; she knew that she had to return, which she did, remembering everything about the experience, stressing it 'was real'.

At Hampstead, London, in 1956, a man aged sixty-five years was lying in bed one morning waiting for his usual time of getting up. Suddenly he was aware of leaving his body. While in the air, looking down, he addressed his body saying, 'Poor useless body, you have served your purpose and now I must leave you.' And then a voice of very great authority called out to him, 'Not yet, not yet, the time has not come yet.' And as he states, 'In obedience, I sank back again into my body. Definitely this was not a dream.'[5]

A lady recorded that in 1973, she was 'rather ill with a chest infection and for nine weeks I had a terrible cough'. She was worried in case it was serious, and then one night, she awoke with a start and couldn't move, 'just as if I had been coming too after an operation'. She explains feeling hands moving inside her body, 'all over, very gentle hands'. The next day she told her family about it and said that she felt 'on the mend. I have been super ever since. I am sixty years old and feel like thirty. I don't go to church now but still believe in a supreme power in ourselves.'[6]

Another lady, Hilda Nuttal, from Halifax, Yorkshire, who was not particularly religious, had a similar experience while asleep. Having been ill for a while with a chest problem, she was aware one night of nuns in her bedroom, standing around the bed ministering to her. Again she felt better the next day.

It was 1996 and Mary Wilton, a lady suffering from Alzheimer's disease, although still up and about with help, suddenly sat up in bed one night and happily and clearly told her carer, Elaine, 'I'm going to heaven.' Elaine, astounded, as Mary could usually barely speak and even then not clearly, had only just phoned her daughter (who was abroad at the time on holiday) telling her how well her mother was. Not believing what she had just heard Elaine asked Mary to repeat what she had said. Without any hesitation and again quite happily and clearly, Mary repeated, 'I'm going to heaven,' then settled down to sleep. She passed away only days later.

• • •

Children describe having the same sort of near-death experiences and out-of-body experiences as adults, telling about things they couldn't possibly have known. The experiences are universal, not explained by science or by any of the five senses. And then, of course, there are strange things that happen with no apparent explanation or reason. Stories that defy being called anything other than 'incredible'. Stories that go beyond coincidence.

We wonder at the amazing story of the doctor and the painting. A landscape painting had hung in his house for years. No one knew where the scene was painted but it was often speculated on. Finally the painting was relegated to the garage. Both the doctor and his wife were regular travellers, jetting all over the world, but one trip really astonished them. They knew that this was their first visit to this particular place, yet could not shake off the feeling that they had been there before. This bothered them for most of the holiday, but it was not until the end of their stay that they realised they were at the scene of the painting! They were hardly able to wait to confirm this, but did so on arrival back home. Needless to say, the picture was immediately taken out of the garage and restored to its former glory, still a talking point, only this time, even more so.

We can only marvel at such incidents and so many that happen in an ordinary, workday environment, but they make us think! The headmaster of a large comprehensive school, a science specialist, was a man in no way given to fanciful thoughts or imagination. But one day he found himself having to confide to a trusted colleague an experience that had left him completely baffled and uneasy. He told how he was walking along the school corridor, which he did several times a day, glancing through the windows of the classrooms as he passed, and, on this occasion, particularly noticed a girl sitting there who had left the school months previously. Registering surprise at this, as he was not aware of her return and in any case, he would have been consulted before she was re-admitted, he simply put it to the back of his mind. As he did not see her again, or hear her name mentioned by any of the staff, he decided he had simply (unusual though it was for him), imagined her presence. Days later, he was quite incredulous when the girl and her mother arrived at the school office to apply for her re-admittance, having just returned to the area.

It was World War I. A soldier from the USA survived his troop ship being torpedoed off the coast of France; he lost all his possessions. In America after the war, standing by the seashore near Brooklyn, he found a shaving-brush cast up by the tide. It had an army number on the back. It was his.

Barbara, from Woodley in Berkshire, accidentally flushed her antique bracelet down the toilet. Months later she was in a jeweller's shop when a man walked in with a bracelet to be valued; he had found it while working in a sewer. It was the very one she had lost.

Linked in with strange incidents are ones of positive sightings from the other side, but with no obvious meaning – except perhaps to prove 'we are never alone'.

Rachael Thomas, a young English lady, is a holiday representative working overseas with American tourists. Her story happened in 2003. She was walking home from work (Can Cun in Mexico), at her usual time, about nine p.m., down a road which is a short cut and one she uses regularly.

There was no one on either side or in front of me, when a family appeared. It was at the cross roads, and I could see them clearly in the car headlights that had come up behind me. There was a bald-headed man with a child on his back and other children around him. He wore what looked like a robe made of hessian tied in the middle with a rope. The little family crossed the road in front of me and just disappeared. I was so amazed I looked all over for them, this way and that, but they had completely disappeared.

Rachael continued with the observation that, 'It was as natural as if there are spirit people there all the time, around us, but suddenly an infra red light comes on enabling us to see them – to "tune in".'

Not long before this experience, Rachael had suffered from a broken romance and was still trying to come to terms with it all. Could it be in some crises, some trauma, distress or worry, that in this heightened state of awareness, we are more sensitive and therefore, as many would suggest, more susceptible to imagining things? Or is it that this heightened state of awareness opens a door into some other state of consciousness that we have been privileged to witness? There is absolutely no doubt in Rachael's mind that she saw the family, with every detail of the encounter as clear as if it was yesterday. When people have a paranormal experience, they know they have had one!

Fate, coincidence, superstition, all part of the puzzle, the mystery of life, and it is often only when something extraordinary or sadly, 'devastating', happens, that we pause to think. Lisa decided it was time her mother got over her superstition about walking over the railway crossing at Moots Lane in Essex. Her father had been killed there eleven years previously, and when they were out walking one day in August 1995, Lisa stood on the crossing and tried to encourage her mother over. A train suddenly approached and hit Lisa, killing her instantly.

With no obvious reason as to how, or why, such tragedies happen, it is also undeniably true that other strange incidents can bring comfort (as in the case of Peter and the numbers), and upliftment.

Stuart Spencer's wife died in 1997 and it was in 2000 that his daughter gave him a 1,000-piece jigsaw puzzle of a paddle-steamer on the Norfolk Broads. Fitting the last piece into place, he recognised the figure sitting at the stern as none other than his sadly missed wife, snapped unawares while on holiday, six years earlier.

As if to lighten the load on this oft times sad journey of ours, there are many amusing things that happen; funny, incredible and true. So whence the source? Tony loved his dad, and when he passed to the other side of life, proudly wore his gold watch, that is, until it insisted on falling to pieces on his wrist. Secured firmly in place, there was no apparent reason for this happening, and both Tony and his girlfriend Trish enjoyed many a good laugh because of it. One night, the watch again firmly in place, Trish's father questioned, 'What's all this I've been hearing about a watch then?' and Tony duly pulled up his coat sleeve. As they looked, it once again disintegrated (sarcasm turning to surprise).

Jimmy Brown sells wallpaper from a market stall at Blyth, Northumberland, and will never forget the day – but let us hear the story from his customer Janet; the story of the wallpaper that jumped.

Janet had finished decorating her bungalow and was pleased with the result except for one noticeable patch on the main bedroom wall. She was short by half a strip of paper and knew she had bought the last roll of that particular pattern and colour. Talking to Jimmy about it, he insisted he would be able to find another roll at one of the warehouses on his travels.

Weeks passed, each one taking Janet back to Jimmy's stall, but no luck, no wallpaper. Bright and breezy, Jimmy was confident that he would come across the pattern again, but through time Janet became despondent and disappointed. One day, going into the bedroom, she looked at the wall and said out loud, 'Oh doesn't it look a mess, such a mess?' She sat on the edge of the bed and thought, 'What am I going to do? I can't afford to re-paper it and I haven't got the time or the energy anyway,' then decided she would just have to make the best of it.

Janet started to avoid Jimmy's stall on her weekly visit to the market and gradually forgot about the whole thing until one day, walking round the stalls as usual, she heard a voice calling to her. It was Jimmy. Both excited and agitated, he called out to her, 'Here, come and see.' His story was hard to believe. Jimmy had paid his usual visit to a huge warehouse in Manchester, one he frequented along with others. On this particular day, as he strolled along, passing countless shelves stacked with assorted patterns and colours of wallpaper, a roll jumped out of a fixture and landed at his feet. He told how, astounded, he froze on the spot, then slowly picked it up, seeing immediately that it was the very one he had been hunting for, for weeks; Janet's.

• • •

From amusing to deeply spiritual, contact with the 'unnamed something', the 'universal energy', the 'life force', 'God', can apparently propel us into a different state of awareness where, even if only for one brief moment, we touch upon something we know to be greater and more important than ourselves. A medical person's explanation for such phenomena could include psycho-dynamics, which include psycho-analytical theory, psycho-kinesis, quantum tunnelling, temporal lobe disturbance, and other terms used within the language of physics. Big words, impressive terms, but what do they tell us about so-called paranormal experiences? Science, swathed as it is in academia, and within its own artificial setting, cannot capture the 'truth' of the moment. Perhaps the genius of the musician, the artist, the writer, soaring to great heights in a flow of creativity come close, feeling their inspiration to be as 'not of this world'. But what of those drowning in despair, heart broken, with troubles multiplied to breaking point? – suddenly upheld, led to a chink in the darkness, a light; given an inner sense of hope and peace:

Just when I couldn't bear it anymore, couldn't go on, the phone would ring or the door bell – and once again I was saved...

'Know'. They *know*, without a shadow of doubt, the reality of the 'unnamed something'.

To move on in our thinking and perhaps delve a little more deeply into the meaning of life's experiences, we can question 'reality' itself. What is reality? Is it that all of life's experiences, including dreams, near-death experiences and out-of-body experiences, together make up our reality? Is reality where we are at any given moment in time, the moment of experience; not yesterday, tomorrow, but now? What of when we sleep, while moving in and out of dreams, or when we pass? Is the very moment of experiencing whatever it is we are experiencing our reality?

> *What we call death is not a complete ceasing to be.*
> *Rather it is a transition to another state of living.*[7]

'To another state of living, to another reality.' There are a growing number of doctors who now believe that the patient is often the best source of diagnosis for his or her own illness, the patient having a 'feeling', an inner sense of what is wrong.

An inner sense is something we are all born with, but, it seems, we often fail to realise it, clouded as it is by the constant conditioning of materialism. An inner sense or feeling that, as so many have experienced, can take us to the top of the mountain, or hold us safe when in the depths of despair. A sense that tells us we are never alone, that our little ship does have a guiding star, that no matter how hard our lot, or how sad, there is always an unnamed something, a universal energy, a life force, God – there for us.

And just as most people who have gone through the near-death experience are transformed, becoming more caring, compassionate, spiritual, so too, many who have an out-of-body experience express a feeling of being at one with nature, with all life, the sea, the sky, the rocks, the universe. They report being 'flooded with warmth', having a glowing feeling, a great sense of comfort; touching a depth they have never experienced before, where there are no words to recall the living of that moment; the sweetness of the sensation; the exuberance of 'knowing'; the certainty that all is well and that all will be well.

And so it is, we are assured, when the truth – that we are here and now spiritual beings in a physical body – dawns on us. We understand the message; we glimpse the mystery:

> There are more things in heaven and earth, Horatio,
> Than are dreamt of in your philosophy...[8]

yet marvel still at the sheer magic of it all.

We have read about and perhaps accepted that many strange things do happen in life (we may even by now have recalled some of our own), and if we decide to put some experiences down to coincidence, we remember that a coincidence is God's way of performing a miracle anonymously – so perhaps we are ready to accept the stories of, what Billy Graham calls 'God's Secret Agents'.[9] The stories of the Angels.

Chapter Three

'Be not forgetful to entertain strangers:
for thereby some have entertained angels unawares.'[1]

MRS B WAS PANICKING when a broken boiler threatened to ruin an important dinner party. She looked up a name in the telephone directory and a man arrived and mended the boiler. To use her own words, 'He walked into my lounge, looked around, and said, "Tonight will be good." ' He told her he was her guardian angel, then he left. Mrs B never received a bill for the repair, and when she tried to find his name in the telephone directory again, the company was not listed.

Apparently seeing an angel can be as ordinary as going to the shops or as mystical as the deepest revelations we read about in the Bible.

It was 1938 and the grim days leading up to the start of the Second World War. No one felt safe, and poverty was the norm. In a small old seaport town, somewhere in the North East of England, lived Norah. Her home was a flat on the ground floor, part of a short terrace of old houses situated in the centre of the town. Norah's husband Jack, a merchant seaman, was on duty at sea and she had no idea when he would return. She had two older children to look after, and a sickly baby of a few months to care for. The tiny girl – the mother called her 'miracle baby' as she weighed only four pounds at birth – had developed serious chest problems.

One day the priest called, and he was so concerned at how poorly the baby was that he hurried away to seek a doctor. That night, as she lay in her cot, having difficulty breathing, Norah lay in bed watching her, the cot having been placed at the side of the bed. Suddenly, the room was enveloped in a beautiful perfume, then, astonished, Norah watched as two angels, sweeping wings, widespread, flew over the cot. The baby's breathing immediately improved, she was well, and grew up to become a healthy mother of three.

The appearance of angels signified a change for the better in Norah's baby, but in another incident that happened at about the same time, in the late thirties, the paranormal experience heralded a different outcome.

Once again a mother was anxiously watching over her sick baby as he lay in his cradle. What she described as the most wonderful shining light in the shape of a star (could it have been an angel?), appeared and hovered over the cradle. It stayed there for a little while. Then, as she watched, it gradually faded, and as it faded, so the life of the baby gently slipped away.

William Roach, a well-known TV actor who writes and speaks openly about his experiences with 'the other side', gives a simple but moving account of help coming from 'angelic forces' as he describes them, at a time of great need.

> Years ago, after I lost my little girl Edwina at eighteen months, my wife and I were grief stricken and didn't know how we would cope with the funeral. On the morning of the funeral, the smiling face of Edwina appeared surrounded by a golden glow. With her came a feeling of comfort and love. She appeared with the help of angelic forces.

The presence of angels is mentioned in the Bible nearly three hundred times,[2] and as we follow the stories of their appearance, we realise that the message they bring can also apply to present-day situations.

> Jesus said, 'I thank Thee O Father, Lord of Heaven and earth, because thou hast hid these things from the wise and prudent, and hast revealed them unto babes.'[3]

Sitting in the nursery with her six-month-old baby as usual for a quiet hour before her bedtime – about six o'clock – a mother tells of something very special that occurred. They were sitting there, playing and chatting, the baby on her knee, when suddenly she (the baby) became very quiet. She lifted her head and gazed intently across the room at one spot as if someone had just entered and spoken to her. Her little face had an expression of great pleasure. Her eyes were fixed on this 'somebody' and she seemed to be listening for a few minutes and reacting, all the time with the blissful gaze and slight movements of eyes that were shining with pleasure. 'I felt myself breathless, afraid to move my position at all for fear of disturbing or interrupting what was going on. The silence was full of some mysterious atmosphere, then all at once it was over.' This experience happened again on two or more occasions soon afterwards, then no more. The baby grew into a happy, normal, healthy little girl.[4]

• • •

A child sees easily because it is natural, accepting, and innocent. Geoffrey Wright, retired now, will never forget his experience when his grandmother took him to church. He was five years old and he says that while everyone was praying, he saw the figure of a man gradually materialise at the front of the church. 'The man was shining in gold.' Geoffrey started tugging at his grandmother to look, but they were praying, and all had their eyes closed. All she could say to him was, 'Be quiet, be quiet.' He remembered thinking that no wonder they couldn't see the man when they were sitting with their eyes closed.

In May of 2004, Linda Broady, an assistant in a playgroup held in a church hall in Ashington, Northumberland, reported the story of a three-year-old girl. The child was playing with the other children as usual, looked up at an arched window, and said, 'I can see an angel.' Linda, rather taken back at the spontaneity and positive way the remark was made, asked, 'Oh, what colour is it?' to which the child replied, 'It is blue.' There was no picture in the window.

A lady from York remembers:

> When I was seventeen years old my sister aged five years contracted a disease which I also had in a much milder form. Late one night mother rushed downstairs with her in her arms and as she passed my bedroom door, I heard angels singing as though they were at my bedside... 'there's a home for little children above the bright blue sky'. I can hear it yet, needless to say she was dead then. The singing is still as real as ever, perhaps it will leave me now that I have reported it.[5]

No one ever forgets, down to the tiniest detail, when they have seen an angel. Apparently angels can become visible when necessary, but, as Billy Graham tells us: 'Our eyes are not constructed to see them ordinarily any more than we can see the dimensions of a nuclear field, the structure of atoms, or the electricity that flows through copper wiring. Our ability to sense reality is limited[6] (but nature has this special 'sense'). Seeing the vision, and feeling that wondrous warm feeling of comfort, of all-embracing pure love – a glowing feeling, and often one of being surrounded by a beautiful light, is rare. Many such experiences happen in childhood and are so spontaneous and joyful they are a privilege for us to share.

A lady living in North Wales was twelve years old when it happened. While running down a hill near her home, she chanced to look up and saw four angels right above her head, with wings and in white, high up in the sky.[7]

Another lady tells us she was about nine years old and at Sunday school when she saw angels around the vicar. He was a very old man and died soon after. She remembers the incident didn't seem odd at the time but since then she has questioned it. 'Perhaps experiences are found to be useful,' she writes (she has had other small, near-death experiences); 'they give us awareness.'[8]

The words from the Bible, *'He will give his angels charge of you, to guard you in all your ways'*, apply very much to the story from a lady who, in New York State, as a child of seven, was out in a 'terrible fierce thunder storm with falling trees, poles and electric wires'. She was going home, only a few blocks away from her day school.

> As I passed a doorway on my right side, I felt a hand firmly but gently on my left arm just above the elbow and I was guided to this sheltered spot. There were a few other people already taking advantage of this doorway (one woman was hysterically calling out to God to save her). When I asked who had brought me in out of the storm each one looked at me as if noticing me for the first time.[9]

The following well-documented story of an amazing life-saving experience, with angels playing a major part, also comes from America, and concerns a three-year-old boy.

Gavin was revived after being trapped underneath an automatic garage door that had crushed the sternum above his heart. He endured endless surgery over the following month, then one afternoon, after awakening from an afternoon nap, called out to his mommy that he had something important to tell her.

She sat beside him on the bed then, in his own child's language, he tried to describe to her exactly what had happened to him after the accident.

He told how heavy the garage door was and how much it had hurt him being stuck under it. He said he had called out to her, then the 'hurt' was so bad he could hardly bear it and started to cry. And then the 'birdies' came.

'Birdies,' exclaimed his mother! Gavin clearly described the whooshing sound as they flew into the garage and took care of him. 'One of them got you and told you I got stuck under the door.' His mother, pressing him to describe the 'birdies', listened incredulously as he described them as 'beautiful'. Dressed all in white, some in green and white, he told her that they had said to him the 'baby would be all right'.

'What baby?'

'The baby lying on the garage floor,' he answered.

She realised that, not having the language to say 'angels', he was describing them as 'birdies' because of their wings and that they were flying. He described her 'opening the garage door, running to the baby and telling him not to move'. On hearing this, she nearly collapsed, as she had indeed knelt beside Gavin; seeing his crushed chest and unrecognisable features, she knew that he was dead.

He described how she had looked up and around her and whispered, 'Please don't leave us, Gavin, please stay if you can.' Hearing him tell her the words she had spoken, she realised that his spirit had left the body and he had looked down on it as she knelt there.

Gavin tried to tell of how he went on a trip far, far away, with the birdies – 'they were so pretty' – struggling to find words to describe his experience. The birdies had told him he must come back and tell everyone about them, and when they brought him back, he described seeing a big fire truck and an ambulance, and a man bringing the baby out on a white bed. The birdies said he must go with the ambulance but they would be near. And then a bright light had appeared. He described it as so bright and so warm he loved it. Someone was in the bright light and put their arms around him saying they loved him, but that he had to go back. 'You have to play baseball and tell everyone about the birdies.'

Gavin never forgot his story and told everyone about it, including complete strangers, who were astounded at this young child remembering such detail and having a vocabulary way beyond his years. His parents related never having been the same since that day, and prayed that they never would be!

• • •

Anne Watkins from Wales asks the question, 'Did I meet an angel?' When on holiday alone in Turkey, she had an extraordinary experience.

> It was 1998. I was on holiday in Turkey and, as usual, travelling alone. I had visited friends in Odemis who had rung from their home to reserve a seat for me on the coach to Balikesir. Emine put me on a bus near their house that would drop me at the bus station in Izmir. There I transferred to a dolomus for Ege station. A journey that should have taken thirty minutes took nearer an hour. Already things were starting to go wrong.

I do not speak Turkish so upon arrival at the depot showed my piece of paper with destination, time etc but it resulted only in blank faces. My bag was heavy, the rain torrential and I waded out, calf deep, to the main road. I showed the soggy piece of paper to a policeman who attempted to speak German, which I do not understand. He directed me over the road, along a street and up a hill.

Upon showing my disintegrating piece of paper to a man with a child, he put me on a bus. It was packed. There was some general discussion about the details on the paper and we set off. I was surprised that they would not accept my fare and presumed we were on our way to Balikesir. I was horrified when the bus pulled up at a garage on the motorway and put me off, giving my case and instructions to a teenager in the forecourt. At the counter the garage attendant was disinterested in the message from the teenager and my piece of paper. It was 12pm. I was completely lost; did not know where I was or how to get to my next stop.

Then a young man spoke. He was Turkish but unlike the Turks I had met on my journey he wore western trousers, polished shoes, a white, ironed shirt, and was clean-shaven. He asked if I was all right and could he help. I described my predicament and he advised me that all buses that pass here go to Istanbul. To my objection that that was not where I wanted to go, he explained that all buses for Istanbul pass through Balikesir.

The man led me out of the garage, across the motorway

and flagged down a coach. I ran along the hard shoulder and got on. It all happened so quickly that I am not sure I even thanked him properly.

I collapsed into a seat near the rear of the bus. Paid my fare, removed my soaking shoes, wrung out my dripping socks and began to eat a bar of chocolate. The driver's assistant started to fuss about moving me to the front of the vehicle. It seemed completely unnecessary as there were only a few passengers but I felt obliged to do as requested and sat, as shown, in seat number two. I don't know if he had sensed my reluctance to move but returned with his clip board to show me seat 2 reserved in my name. Time of departure 11.30 am. Time of arrival 14.30. It was my bus!!!

I would arrive at the pre-arranged time and friends would be there to meet me. I immediately attributed this miraculous coincidence to the work of my Guardian Angel but now I wonder…was the English speaking gentleman in a white shirt an angel?

But what is an angel? Angel means messenger, and angels are believed to be messengers from God. Presumably then, Angels are one of the ways the 'unnamed something', the 'universal energy', the 'life force', 'God', reaches out to us with love, help, comfort, whatever our need – proving to us we are never alone. The Bible tells us we all have a guardian angel, from the moment of conception; *'He has given His Angels charge concerning thee, to keep thee in thy ways.'* And they may take any form apparently, as they speed towards us in answer to prayer – or thought.

Sandra Scott attended a Sunday evening service but afterwards had to walk back home alone, along a very dark lane. She hoped that an angel might be sent to be with her, and at that moment, was joined by a big black dog that walked with her until she reached her front door. She had never seen the dog before and never saw it again. Angels disguised as dogs?[10]

A man who ignored a strong urge, a strong impression – could it have been his guardian angel trying to impress him – *'When Joseph awoke from sleep, he did as the angel of the Lord commanded him';* – had to face the awful consequences of not heeding to his 'inner voice'.

> It was a Sunday in late '44. The Germans were sending their rockets (V2s) over London. I had a young lady friend staying at my house and we decided to go to the cinema. We came out, and walked to the bus terminal. I had a strong impression to run for the bus; I could see it standing a couple of hundred yards away with the lights on and no queue, but I had this urge to run! I didn't, and I was suddenly blown into some empty shops that were by our side while we were walking for the bus. The girl who was with me was killed while I was only slightly hurt. Regaining consciousness, in the middle of screaming, injured people, I saw the undamaged bus standing where it had been before the rocket fell, lights still on.[11]

To return to more recent times (with guardian angels, it seems, in 'operation' as always), and about the year 2000, Tony Jones, a young lad of seventeen years of age, living near Newcastle-On-Tyne, started seeing shadows and glimpses of what he felt to be a boy of about his own age in his bedroom. He was not afraid; in fact, when he did finally talk about this, he said it was a nice feeling. His mother felt it would be his guardian angel – he was once saved from having a bad accident going up an escalator and at the time said that he had felt an arm around his shoulder.

A young girl intended to walk home alone, across a field. Suddenly she became aware of an unseen presence watching over her and she heard a voice distinctly say, 'Go back.' The presence became more forceful when she still attempted to cross the field, so she obeyed. A week later, a six-year-old girl, crossing the same field, was molested, raped, and left bleeding in a wagon.[12]

Marion, aged nine or ten years, was out walking by the sea with a friend and two dogs. On the spur of the moment she decided to climb an eroded cliff and ran up to discover it was only a foot wide. The way she ran she should have gone straight over the edge into the sea below, but she was prevented from doing so by being brought to a halt by an 'invisible wall of force' which bounced her away. She was, as she said, 'startled', but remembers thinking, 'There is something there.'[13]

The question can be asked, why were the children in the above incidents 'saved', while one little girl crossing a field was savagely attacked? I received a letter while researching for this work in which the writer asks the same sort of question.

I understand you are interested in accounts from people regarding 'Guardian Angels'. There are, of course, no such beings! And anyone who says they have one are rather arrogant – assuming that they are 'special'! Millions of people – very often *very religious* people have suffered horrendous treatment and hideous deaths, yet, where were these mythical guardian angels when they were desperately needed?

How can the question posed in the letter be answered? Life is a mystery, and there is often no explanation in our understanding for what happens. But it is believed that there is a reason for everything, a purpose; and it seems that it is often through experiencing the deepest tragedy that we are moved to 'go within' and seek answers, meanings; trying to make sense of this sojourn of ours. And it also seems that the best proof is the truth we discover for ourselves, when our inner being, ever struggling to be heard, speaks to us, and amazingly, we just 'know'...not all the answers, not how to avoid the slings and arrows life flings at us, but how to cope with them; how to put a guard around ourselves, to understand and know that somehow, from somewhere, we are protected – loved beyond our understanding. And that even in the direst situations, when we can hardly bear to think about, say, what a loved one has suffered, we may come to the realisation that they too, in their need, have had protection; have been cocooned in that indescribable love which surpasses all physical conditions. (Cases have been reported where those undergoing horrific ordeals have actually left their bodies at the time of the trauma.)

> Except you see signs and wonders,
> You will not believe.

To see an angel physically, or a man in shining gold, are surely the rare experiences when, to use an old expression, heaven to earth comes down. But examples prove that probably the more usual ways for the 'unnamed something', the universal energy, the life force, God – for the angels to talk to us, are in dreams or in everyday experiences.

> Suddenly a great warmth came over me. I felt loved
> and not alone and that all would be well.

Still in deep, thoughtful mood she spoke of her amazement,

disbelief, at the strength they had to cope, adding, 'It must have come from somewhere.'

Just when I couldn't bear it any more, couldn't go on,
the phone would ring, or the doorbell and once again
I was saved and led into a saner frame of mind.

A class studying angels was asked to look out for angels the following week. Not necessarily angel beings flying around, but incidents, things happening that were in some way special, with perhaps some deep meaning. This particular lady in the class, very depressed at the time, and walking down a street she had walked down a thousand times before, casually glanced up. Above her, looking down, was a stone angel with the sunlight shining all over it. She had never seen it before. Suddenly she felt warm and safe. *'Protected, an indescribable love which surpasses all physical conditions.'*

Karen, a lady from Lancashire, who tells the story of an angel at her shoulder, is a reminder that there is a revival of angel phenomena in our country. The 'angel on my shoulder brooches', the uncountable selection of merchandise depicting angels, the emergence of angel societies, as in America, where they even have their own angel newspaper.

Nevertheless, are there really such beings as those we call angels? Are they not just something we need for assurance, for comfort from time to time, as a child needs a comfort blanket or favourite toy? Are they not simply a figment of the imagination? Karen doesn't think so.

Karen's husband Don, aged thirty-five, had been killed in a car crash eighteen months before her angel experience. She was left to bring up three children and coped the best way she could, but she had her bad days. One of the worst was in the dark days of January after the family's second Christmas without him. She woke up feeling 'down', and knew how hard the day would be, getting the children off to school, doing the chores; everything was such a struggle. Feeling desperate, she forced herself to get on with things and, as she was mopping the floor, she felt a hand on her shoulder. She looked around expecting someone to be there and was surprised to find she was still alone. But she wasn't frightened at all. No words were spoken, but she knew that the hand had said to her, 'Trust.' She knew she had an angel at her shoulder. When asked, 'Why an angel?' she replied, 'Somehow you just know.' She talks about it openly now because, as she says, she has heard so many similar tales, but she admits to being wary of talking about it at first, outside the family.

All religions believe in angels, but sometimes under a different name. The Essenes were a strict religious sect who lived over two thousand years ago. Jesus was thought to have lived amongst them for a time. They believed that in order to achieve wholeness within, it was necessary to harmonise the spiritual with the physical – a belief held firmly today – and that the key to this is daily communion with angels.

Sandra Cresswell from Northumberland, a present-day, well respected and successful practitioner of Reiki Healing, has no doubt at all as to the presence of angels, both in her personal life and in her work as a healer. She spends at least twenty minutes a day in meditation (taught with the Reiki healing technique), in order to be 'in tune' before she begins her work. As Sandra explains, she calls in the healing angels, stressing that she herself is only a channel. The client pulls the energy through the healer (the channel). To quote Sandra, 'Reiki is pure, unconditional love. That is why we are here, to give out love and help each other.' She perceives angels in the traditional way and prays to 'Mother/ Father God', or the divine spirit.[14]

Those who possess insight behold angels with their

spiritual eyes which they experience very often in a *state of wakefulness.*

• • •

One of the most dramatic – still argued about – tales to come out of the First World War was the story of the Angel of Mons. It was 1914 and the small British Expeditionary Force was outnumbered three to one by the Germans. It was believed that a miracle happened during the first onslaught at Mons in Belgium. An angel, or angels, held back the Germans, preventing the British force from meeting certain death. Not believing that there was to be no attack, the troops turned and saw an army of angels between them and the Germans, the German horses, terrified, stampeding in every direction. Many soldiers reported seeing only one huge angel holding back the enemy. But the sighting, confirmed by both sides, seemed to confirm the presence of some force. And when it was reported that German troops refused to charge through a broken point in the British line due to the large number of soldiers, the British were amazed as their records showed no presence of troops in the area.

Although the story of the Angel of Mons has been almost totally discredited many times since those far-off days, and it seems to be almost impossible now to verify the truth, one thing is absolutely certain: the evidence from the nurses in the field hospital at the time. The nurses testified to never having seen such peace, almost happiness, on the faces of the wounded and dying men brought in on that fateful day.

The historian A J P Taylor was so impressed by evidence from the story of Mons that he referred to it in his 1963 history of the First World War as the only battle where *'supernatural intervention was observed, more or less reliably, on the British side'.* But there were countless individual stories of help coming from a 'higher force'.

An ex-soldier from Essex reports his personal experiences while serving in that horrendous battle of the Somme, as a Second Lieutenant. He was sent with other subalterns to make up battalion losses. The night before a planned attack on Ginchy, his company commander was recalled to headquarters and he had to take his place. He led two hundred and fifty men over the top to face heavy artillery fire, sustaining many losses. Seeing no enemy in the village, they occupied a trench where they waited in case of counter-attack. Although this was his first action, he felt no fear, only a sense of not being alone, of a 'presence' with him; he knew nothing could happen to him and even felt happy. Although reduced to sixteen men and three officers the company was in good spirits.

Three days later he saw movements five to six hundred yards away and crawled, under heavy fire from both sides, to see which troops they were. The wonderful presence remained with him and he knew he was protected. The protected feeling was with him in future battles and raids but he has no explanation to offer. The experience has remained with him.[15]

During the Second World War, Captain William Dunbar MM was a prisoner of war held in the mountains of Italy (near Aquila), in the convent of San Spirito. The convent was ancient, and had an old wall – rampart, around it with iron rings, said to be where the Roman Galleons had tied up, as in earlier times it had been an inlet. Every now and again about fifty prisoners would be taken for a walk on the mountain, near the convent, with Italian guards. On this particular day the guards ran away and the prisoners too. Three of them, including the captain, kept together and were plodding on when three German soldiers appeared. The men were terrified and didn't know what to do. The Germans stopped to urinate and the men would have to pass them if they kept walking. Suddenly a voice said to the captain, 'Just walk on.' Amazed, but not doubting what he had heard, he told the others to keep going, which they did. The Germans, engrossed in conversation, ignored them as they walked by. Eventually, peasants gave them clothes and they did reach safety six weeks later.

Doug Halliday, a young service man in the 'sixties, sometimes put out religious tracts from the Bible in the hallway of the barracks. One day he found an ancient self-defence book lying around and picked it up just to scan through it. Two things stuck in his mind. He was putting another tract out one day when a fellow serviceman came in and was really annoyed to find that it was not the padre who was putting these tracts out. He was so annoyed that he struck out and aimed a punch at Doug's jaw. Suddenly remembering the two things he had read in the book on self defence saved him, as he knew how to deflect the blow aimed at his jaw and avert the kicks lashed out at him. Doug claims that it was his guardian angel who saved him that day.

A sudden thought that prevented a tragic accident is how a young lad in the air-training core sees his guardian angel helping him. He was visiting a camp and was taken to look at the jet planes in a hangar. He stood alone on the canopy looking down into the cockpit while the sergeant explained to him about the ejector seat. The sergeant was actually sliding the pin out to show how it worked, when suddenly he stopped, and put it back in, having a sudden thought that he had better check that it was disconnected – which of course it should have been. Acting on his sudden thought prevented a tragic accident.

• • •

There is a belief that we all see or experience the presence of angels – in one way or another. Yet how many times have they come into our lives and we haven't recognised them?

Peter went out and followed [the angel]; he did not

realise that what was happening with the angel's help was real; he thought he was seeing a vision.

Guy James, an American, didn't believe in angels until he had an experience. Since then he says he will often ask, 'Will you guys give me a hand?' and suddenly 'a warmth' comes over him. As we understand, angel means 'messenger', and evidence suggests that they can appear in any shape or form when help is needed, often talking to us when we are asleep, carrying their messages in dreams or prayers. Many people believe prayer brings the angels down. Linda from Lancashire conveys to us the uplift she felt after asking for help at a time of great stress in her life.

> Life was so chaotic. I felt I was going round in circles. I put my hands on the kitchen table and in despair said, 'Please, Lord, take the heavy burden away, I can't go on.' I felt a presence at my side and slowly the burden lifted – there was a force in that room I had never in my life felt before – a great peace came over me and a feeling of utter joy.[16]

White Eagle, a famous spiritual teacher, gives us the following words of comfort;

> Each one of you is accompanied by an illumined soul from the world of light, by a guide, a companion or teacher, and certainly by one who is the affinity of your spirit; for where love is there is no separation.

For where love is, there is no separation. A love transcending all religion. A feeling, an experience, at once so beautiful and compassionate and reassuring, that can apparently lift us out of the terrible plight or heartache engulfing us, and put us in an atmosphere of exhilaration, assurance, certainty that we are not alone. A divine intervention is taking place in our lives and somehow we know that all will be well.

> My husband died as the result of an accident at the age of forty-two years after an extremely happy marriage of eight years. I was left with two small daughters and a son nine months old. I was completely shattered and unable to imagine how I could carry on. I hadn't been brought up with much faith and was, I suppose, what is called a free thinker. Yet could not face the thought of life being entirely pointless, without meaning, which his dying seemed to be to me. I can truly say I was at the bottom of a black pit, knowing that no earthly props were going to help me. One night I was kneeling by my son's cot in great anguish, when suddenly I seemed to be surrounded by and filled with light and warmth and incredible peace. I don't know how long it lasted but I lay down on my bed and slept as I hadn't slept for weeks. In the morning, the feeling of peace was still there. Over the following month, I knew that only God (and my fellow beings through Him) were sustaining me. Once again, when I was kneeling by my bed in great despair, I yet found myself thanking God for what He had given me, which seemed greater to me than the happiness I had lost.[17]

The wonder of witnessing not only the passing of her husband, but also seeing…could it be an angel helper who assisted him?… was a rare, miraculous happening for a lady from Kent.

> My husband died unexpectedly late one night in the bathroom. I went to try and lift him but couldn't. While

I was contemplating who to call for help, I saw the spirit form of my husband get up out of his night clothes, helped by someone unknown to me, all done most discreetly. I will never forget the incident as long as I live and I am grateful to God who has given me the strength and health to bring up my young son to manhood.[18]

To have felt the hand of an angel-helper was the privilege of Tom, a man in deep despair, who tells how the experience changed his life.

Years ago Tom couldn't face the thought of his wife's funeral: 'The horror of standing at the waiting grave while my beloved partner's remains were lowered into the dark earth' – so on his knees he fervently prayed for God to help him through the ordeal. On the day of the funeral he felt strangely different, calm and collected, viewing the proceedings in a detached way as if merely a spectator, yet inwardly dreading the moment at the graveside. At the committal, all stood beside the grave with closed eyes. He felt a strong hand gripping his forearm firmly to steady him, and assumed it was his wife's brother supporting him. When the prayers were over, he opened his eyes and saw his brother-in-law standing ten feet away – with no one else near enough to have touched him. The grip was unmistakeable and he knows he wasn't deceived. Since that day he has been a different man, knowing that for a moment he was in touch with the infinite, the Creator. He says he will remember it until he himself passes 'through the thin veil'.[19]

Quotes have been used from the Bible to show a link between stories, experiences that happened in those far-off days of Bible history, concerning the appearance and help from angels, and present-day manifestations. Perhaps none can be more startling than the comparison between the Bible story of Jacob's ladder

– Jacob dreamed of a ladder set on earth, the top of it reaching to heaven, with angels ascending and descending – and the experience of a nurse from Pennsylvania.

My experience happened when I was seventeen years old, about a week after my daughter's birth. She was born at home, and the doctor ran into problems. He finally had to use forceps to take the baby. I was very ill afterwards, so they sent me to the hospital.

I was there three days and they wanted to operate. My husband was against this, so he took me home – although I was so ill that I was not able to sit up in bed. It was a Sunday afternoon. He took a taxi and had to carry me in his arms like a baby.

By the time I got home, it seemed that I got strength – where from, I do not know. But I got out of the cab and walked into the house, up to our third floor apartment. I changed the bed the way that I wanted it. I then undressed and got into bed. I felt wonderful. I had never had a feeling like that before, and never since.

My family and neighbours were all there because they were dumbfounded to see the miraculous change that had come over me. Then, just as though there was someone talking to me, a voice told me that I was going to die and that I should let my husband and family know.

So I called them altogether in the room. I held my husband's hand and said to them, 'You must all prepare to meet your God because I am now going to meet mine.'

I felt so peaceful, I didn't have a pain. And when I left the hospital only about three hours before, I was racked with pain. It seemed that I went off in a trance of some kind. While I was in this state, I had a vision.

It seemed that all these angels came from heaven and, holding hands, they formed a stairway reaching all the way up to heaven. It seemed that as I ascended these stairs up to heaven, I knew everything that was going on in my home. My family and neighbours were crying and my husband was kneeling at the bed, begging God to please spare me for the baby's sake.

I kept going up this stair of angels' hands until I reached heaven. When I reached the top, there was a great mist before the door, and an angel said to me, 'That mist is your family's prayers for your return. Why don't you ask the Lord to let you come back to raise your child?'

When I went through the mist, I could see this person sitting on a throne, surrounded by this mist. I said, 'Lord, please let me go back and raise my child.' He did not reply but took my hand and turned me around and led me back to the stairs to descend. In the meantime, I was out so long that the family was making plans for the undertaker and sending telegrams. When I came to, shouting and singing, I am sure you can imagine what kind of a day that was. I am seventy now.[20]

• • •

Help from angelic forces, divine intervention, angelic intervention;

accounts of such incidents are endless and never cease to amaze in their diversity.

A grandmother lay sleeping near her grandchild. She often spent hours at night in prayer and so was sensitive to the spiritual realm. As she slept on this particular night, she was aroused suddenly by something, and when she looked up, she saw this strange creature, 'bound up in light but with a human form'. The being, which she identified as an angel, said nothing, but pointed urgently towards the room where the woman's grandchild lay sleeping. Immediately going to the baby's room, she was horrified at what she saw. The baby had been given a glass bottle of milk during the night, but it had cracked, and a blade of glass, like a knife, was resting precariously against the child's throat. If he had moved, it would have been fatal. This woman fervently believed that her grandchild's life had been saved by angelic intervention.[21]

· · ·

Can it be that angels are sometimes used to prophesy? A scientist claims that he doesn't believe in life after death, but he reported, 'When I was ten years old, I would wake up at night crying because something told me my mother would die when I became eighteen. She died the week after my eighteenth birthday.'

There are endless stories of help in the prevention of accidents through some higher intervention, and Doreen Atkins, from London, gives her remarkable account of two such occasions.

I had just started serious riding lessons at the age of twenty-one, in 1967, and the riding school was having an open day which they did every year so that all the classes could show off their progress. This was my first open day and we all had to stand with our horses along with our class, waiting to go on. It was a grey, chilly, windy day in spring and this can make a horse jittery and restless. I was standing behind my horse, ready to ride but one should never stand directly behind a horse, restless or not. I stood what I thought was a good distance away – just in case – because they can kick out so fast it is quicker than a human reaction to move, this is for the normally one-legged kick back. So I stood shivering, perhaps from nerves more than anything, a good safe distance away but there was an open space to the right of me, nothing in sight, just acres of reeds, brush grass, lovely, when all of a sudden in my right ear, a few inches away, I heard the word 'Doreen', my name. It was so sharp and harsh, like a telling-off whisper when you were doing wrong as a kid, and this in such a quiet place, it made me jump. I turned my head to look and at that exact moment – and I mean exact in the motion of turning, I saw and felt the hair on my left temple move as I saw a horse's two legs come past my eyes. I felt the draught, my fringe moved, a horse's left hind leg had moved my fringe. If I had not heard my name and turned my head, my temple would have been smashed, there is no doubt about it. I would have died with my skull caved in. I looked to my right and there was not a soul in sight. The horse had kicked out both legs so they would cover a greater distance than just one leg.

My second experience was about twenty years later when I was standing at a crossing outside Woolworth's on Camden High Street. I was lost in thought, waiting to cross the road and as I saw movement on the other side, people starting to cross, I stepped out on to the road, just one step, then I heard the same telling-off voice call 'Doreen', in my right ear. I pulled/stepped back and as I did so a motor cycle whizzed past me, I actually felt the draught on my legs. If I had not stopped and moved back I could have had a serious accident. The voice was so sudden, my mind went back to that day at the riding school and how I had been saved then. It was the same voice. My friends all call me Dor, only my parents called me Doreen, so it is kind of a formal name.

Most unusually, Clare writes, she got off her bicycle, outside a village in Kent, and walked with it, just before a main road junction where, as she reached it, two cars crashed. Though showered with glass and a buckled wheel, she escaped unhurt but she feels that if she 'had not been guided by God', she would have been caught in the midst of the crash. Clare feels that God walks with her daily. She had the 'sight', or some special awareness of nature around her; bright, standing out, more real, more alive, a feeling of knowing everything and being at one with the universe; a feeling of ecstasy – in which the sunlight and sky and all the lovely scenery became one great golden light. She felt she had to go to confirmation classes and phoned the vicar at just about the time they were going to start. She did not question that God had told her to do this. On the morning of her first communion, as she knelt at the altar rail, a tall golden figure stood on the north side of the altar. She believes it was an angel.[22]

The following awesome account of a near disaster one fine day makes thrilling reading, and gave dozens of people 'food for thought' as they realised just how lucky they had been. But was it luck, or was there perhaps 'something else'?

It was a busy Bank Holiday by the seaside in Devon. The cliff top and the beach below were packed with people out for the day enjoying it all. Pam and Ray were preparing lunch, when suddenly, they saw a runaway tractor hurtling down the grassy slope towards dozens of holidaymakers lying across its path. The man at the wheel began to zig-zag across the slope trying to avoid the people, even though the tractor was gathering speed. It reached the edge of the cliff and shot over. Pam and Ray's only thought was to rush to be with this man who had saved so many lives, staying with the tractor to steer it away from the crowd. They rushed down the path, along with others, to find that it had landed on an empty car. No one was hurt and Pam ran up to those standing around calling, 'Where is he?' But no one knew what she was talking about. They were adamant there hadn't been a driver. Half an hour was spent searching the undergrowth, convinced that he had been thrown from his seat. Then the driver, the real driver who had left the engine running while he got off to open a gate, turned up. Several other people had seen the mysterious driver but instead of an atmosphere of spookiness, a lingering after-taste of supernatural fear, the happy afternoon which followed was marked by, as other people who have had an angelic experience describe, a tremendous feeling of peace and love.

• • •

Glennyce Eckersley is an author who has written five books on the subject of angels. Her recent publication is the paperback, *Teen Angel*. Glennyce feels that people are drawn to angels because they don't have enough spirituality in their lives. She suggests that with the reduction of numbers going to church, and school assemblies being secular, youngsters are growing up with no spiritual input, 'there is a spiritual vacuum'. They want to know if there is something else. And yet in spite of this serious lack of, maybe 'formal' spirituality, it is surprising how many people are still ready to acknowledge openly, and give thanks to an unseen force, a guardian angel, who they have no doubt has saved them.

Mandy Davis, aged thirty-nine, is certain her dead husband David has become her guardian angel, and has saved her life through warnings, during diabetic attacks. An occupational health worker, Mandy tells of there being no signs before her blood sugar drops. 'I could slip into a coma, but every time I've reached that point Thomas has always woken me.' Thomas is her nine-year old son who was only nine months old when his dad died. 'It's something he's always done. He shouts out, "Mum, Mum," or shakes me. Thomas just instinctively turns up, there is something waking him at important times.' Mandy can't find any other explanation for why he would wake up. She stresses that when she has an attack she doesn't make any sound, and anyway, his room is on the other side of the house. She has had other small experiences, and ends her account with the statement, 'I used to think once you were dead you were dead, but not now.'

Saved by an angel? Nicky, thirteen, was saved from drowning after a mystery figure lifted her out of the water at Bispham, near Blackpool, a few years ago. Nicky suffers from spina bifida, and the accident happened when her wheelchair plunged into a deep pond. Her mother raced back to where she had left her daughter to see a huge man hoisting her out of the water with one hand and her wheelchair with the other. He placed them both on the bank as she dashed over to hug Nicky. Then she turned to thank him, but he had gone. There were no footprints and, as Chris, her mother, explains, 'As a man he was so solid he couldn't have just disappeared. To me he was an angel. One minute he was there, the next gone.'

Doreen James, thirty-four, from Glasgow, has always believed in angels, but the first time she had to put them to the test was when she was involved in a high-speed car smash.

She was driving alone on a motorway when a tyre blew on her car and she veered off the road and hit a tree, yet she was cut from the wreckage with barely a mark. Doreen tells of driving along when a voice in her head told her to 'pull over'. She ignored it, but when the voice told her to take her glasses off, she did, wondering why.

> The next minute the car veered out of control. I left the road and was bumping over fields at some speed. Then a tree stump zapped into view right in front of me. I couldn't miss it, I yelled, 'Please help me, angels.'

> I was whooshed out of my body in an instant. I was above it, looking down at this car at the moment of impact. Then I was thrown back into myself. I was upside down and skidding along on the car roof and I remember thinking, 'Thank God for the airbag.' I could feel it enveloping me all round, cushioning me.

Doreen was trapped for an hour while emergency services worked to cut her free. It was only then that she realised that the car she was travelling in had *no airbag*. But apart from a bit of whiplash, and a small scratch on her hand, she was fine. The car was a write-off. No one could believe she had walked away from it alive.

• • •

The last contributor to this chapter on angels, Tommy Wilkinson, from the north, calls his communication 'a visitation', and it happened about eighty years ago.

My mother was on her deathbed with double pneumonia and in a coma. Years later, she told me that despite the coma, she was conscious of events around her and she could hear relatives arranging her funeral. At a vital moment, I entered, took hold of her hand in mine and bursting into tears, pleaded, 'Mammy, don't leave me, I love you so much.' I was about three or four years old. She told me it was then that she found herself in a well-lit place with an atmosphere of a pleasant summer day. An angel appeared and, taking my mother's hand, said, 'Your little boy has made such an eloquent appeal that we have decided to let you live. Peace be with you.' The crisis over, she made a full recovery and from that day she never saw a doctor for fifty years, till she was in a road accident. I was holding her hand when she died on the eve of her ninety-seventh birthday. She was a very caring parent and I have never known her to tell a lie.

• • •

'Never known her to tell a lie.' Fitting words with which to end this chapter. Our experience can be as ordinary as the one told to me by a young woman who said that she had encountered angels in a vivid dream, not having thought about them previously. The following week she was drawn to notice a talk on the radio about angels and went straight out to buy the book. Becoming 'aware', she had a couple of small signs that told her angels were around. Or the experience can be as startling as the seven-foot angel who appeared at the bottom of a sun-bed! (This story to follow in the chapter on God's Magic.)

Angels as guides; angels as messengers; angels to strengthen. In difficult times, have you ever had a sudden surge of upliftment,

1 *Mr & Mrs Thomas Newton standing in front of the coal-house door, Northumberland.*

2 Nelson Emmerson, soldier seen proudly wearing the uniform of the Coldstream Guards. See below for a more unusual appearance of this photograph!

3a) Snapshot photograph of Nelson's sister-in-law taken on a coach trip in the early 'sixties. His spirit extra appears on the snapshot.

3b)   Same snapshot but with the spirit extra encircled.

4 Orbs – lights photographed underneath Edinburgh Castle, 2003.

5 Heidi's mum with angel wings.

6 Young girl in fire that swept through the old town hall of Wem, Shropshire.

of courage, confidence, that just seemed to 'happen', to come from nowhere, and with it the certainty that, despite everything, all would be well?

> Again one in human form touched me and strengthened me. He said, 'Do not fear, greatly beloved, you are safe. Be strong and courageous.'[23]

Angels as protectors;

> I am going to send an angel in front of you, to guard you on the way...[24]

Angels with God-given powers;

> [Peter and the angel] came before the iron gate leading into the city. It opened for them of its own accord...[25]

Angels: does it matter how they appear, if we are fortunate enough to be able to accept that one has come to us? As a thought, in a dream; seeing them with spiritual eyes or physical eyes; shimmering in a haze of heavenly love; dazzling with a radiance not of this world; splendid in robes of white or green or blue; or in the guise of a black dog. In whatever way we may or may not perceive angels, does it matter? – as long as the message, the great truth, the unshakeable conviction is there; that we are not alone. Seemingly, angels come through love, with a message of love, urging us to love one another. To reinforce in us the wisdom that love is essential to all life; that genuine love solves all problems, and that unconditional love is our inheritance from the 'unnamed something', the 'universal energy' the 'life force', 'God'.

In reading and listening to the stories of others, we are, hopefully, opening our minds, 'tuning in' to the feasibility (if we haven't already accepted it) that 'yes', there is something there. Something we may have only 'touched' on, something we may have yet to touch on. But to countless people, it is there; as real, and as much ours, as the sky at night, and the dawn of another day. Perhaps we should go forward in our lives with the philosophy of the English painter, Sir Edward Coley Burn-Jones, who wrote in a letter,

> The more materialistic science becomes, the more angels I shall paint: their wings are my protest in favour of the immortality of the soul.[26]

When we start looking seriously, with an open mind, maybe then we will see.

Chapter Four

'I was suffering with shock, and when I was taken to the mortuary, I was in a state of collapse, wondering what was facing me and how horrible it would be. Before I went through the door, I said a little prayer and asked God to help me. Immediately all fear left me, I stopped trembling and walked straight to where he was. The peace that was all around I shall never forget.... Such is the power, "The Power of Prayer".'

AS A CHILD, PAUL somehow acquired a prayer box, and it stood on a shelf near his bed for years. It was a red cardboard box, measuring about five by eight inches, the lid, supported at each end by ribbons, opened to reveal rows of tightly rolled scrolls on each of which was written a prayer or 'message'. Flexible tweezers were stationed on top of the scrolls (prayers), and were used to pick out a prayer at random; the idea being that if you had a problem and needed guidance, to say a prayer asking for help, and the advice would be there for you in the words of the scroll (chosen at random). And it worked. The last time Paul remembers using it was as a young man, at a particularly bleak time in his life when, devastated, he could see nothing but darkness ahead. His prayer/message read, 'The darkest hour is just before the dawn.' A little prophesy that, he says, proved to be true.

Many people open the Bible or other inspirational book at random and regard the words that first meet their gaze as an answer. There are prayer wheels, each turn being a prayer; prayer mats on which devotees humbly kneel; prayer cards, rosary beads, and many more artefacts used in the devotional act of prayer. But for those of us not familiar with such things, the very idea of prayer being perhaps 'foreign' to us, what is it? What is prayer? Prayer is simply our own personal, sincere communication with ...the 'unnamed something', the 'universal energy', the 'life-force', 'God'. And the fact that prayer does work, and that it is a power available for us to use freely, anywhere and at any time (so often a lifeline for those in distress) is awesome.

The Essenes, a religious sect who lived over two thousand years ago (mentioned in a previous chapter), taught that to achieve wholeness within, it is necessary to harmonise the spiritual with the physical, and that the key to this is daily communion, or prayer. Early man – who also knew the power of dreams – projected prayers or 'thoughts' to the 'Great Spirit', evidenced for him in the sun or some other manifestation of nature.

We, in the Northern hemisphere, are directly descended from the Celtic peoples whose ancient religion, Druidism was about belief in supernatural worlds. The Druids had a rich supernatural life with a lot of interaction (a sending out of thoughts/prayers) between the living and the dead. They celebrated the presence of the dead, who were believed to protect the lives of the living, and used monuments to celebrate the journey from life to death. (The Romans suppressed the Druid priests. They worried about them because they had no fear of death, and the Romans were not able to understand this).

Thoughts are a form of prayer, and we are advised to be careful how we think, how we choose our words. The author Ralph Waldo Trine, in his book *In Tune With The Infinite*, stresses the power of thought as being the main spring of all that comes into our lives, bringing into play the law of 'cause and effect'. (The eternal law of cause and effect is in perpetual operation and controls the lives of all of us.)

Trine tells us:

> Each is building his own world. We both build from within and we attract from without. Thought is the force with which we build, for thoughts are forces. Like builds like and like attracts like.[1]

He continues, '*In the degree that thought is spiritualised* [coming from the higher self], *it becomes more subtle and powerful in its workings.*' Apparently thoughts/prayers will be answered, but often in a different way to what we expect, the answer maybe requiring a different interpretation. It is interesting to observe however, that many people who do have their prayers answered in a different way (to what they expected), and who are disappointed or even in despair at first, soon seem to realise that the unexpected answer proved to be the right one. (A mass of events that at the time appear pointless and stupid, when viewed in retrospect often form a definite pattern necessary to bring about a certain event.) And they discover that the 'power', the 'guiding force', 'God', had indeed led them onto what was best, after all.

Recently recognised as what a newspaper headline called a mystic message, hidden in the middle of the Bible, 'It is better to trust in the Lord than to put confidence in man.' This was taken from Psalm 118, verse 8. While in another verse from the Bible, Luke 18 v.1, we are advised to 'Pray and do not be afraid': advice perhaps not easy to follow, especially when things look 'black' for us, as a young American found out when he was in trouble.

After stealing a very minor item (it was in the 'sixties), he was horrified to find himself locked in a cellar while the police were called. Anxious to avoid the painful embarrassment to his parents, frenzied, tearful, he cried to God for help several times until he was silenced by a voice (though he doesn't know whether he heard it or only felt it), which reassured and calmed him. Since the incident, he says he has felt the same reassurance on several occasions. He feels he is part of something bigger – a Divine Force – that he is 'just a speck', but a part, just the same.[2] Prayer, in whatever form, heeds neither time nor boundaries, as a lady in Oxfordshire discovered. Her husband was undergoing a serious operation that the medical staff didn't think he'd survive. She had been told to wait quietly at home. Suddenly, something compelled her to go to church where she prayed that God would guide the surgeon's hand; later, she discovered that at the same moment she was praying, the surgeon had felt unable to complete the operation, but suddenly got the strength to do so.[3]

We are persuaded that man is a spiritual being in a physical body, and the spiritual side, the real you and me, will always and 'naturally' turn (in prayer) to that 'unnamed something', 'God', in time of need:

> Sedated for two days after the terrible shock of her husband dying in his chair in front of her, the third night she prayed earnestly that she could see him once more. Towards morning, she woke and heard the door bell ring, and saw a shadowy man open it…her husband was standing outside asking for her. He hugged and kissed her but didn't say anything. She told him she loved him and felt three great sobs within him before he faded away. She doesn't know if this was the answer to her prayer.[4]

Turning to prayer in time of need is the same, and has been the same since time began. Miraculous stories from the Bible and from history – in the fifteenth century we read how Lorenzo the Magnificent, of the powerful Medici family, knew the 'force of prayer',[5] – tell us it was always so. Then and now. Ever present, ever faithful, ever sure.

Here is testimony to the power of prayer given by a British doctor, then in her mid-forties, working in West Africa.

I was working as a woman doctor in a remote mission hospital in West Africa at the time. For a variety of reasons, one other MO and I were temporarily the only doctors in a 160-bed hospital with a large outpatient department. The other doctor suddenly became acutely ill and had to be off duty for ten days.

It looked an impossible situation but had to be faced. I prayed that I might somehow be made adequate. The thought came at once that, as it was manifestly impossible to examine the patients in the wards as one would normally do, at least I could touch each one with an unspoken prayer for healing. This I did, unobtrusively, in the guise of feeling the pulse, made a snap diagnosis of the new patients and ordered treatments.

In the outpatients department one of the sisters saw the old patients; I saw the numerous new cases and dealt with emergency surgery. In this way we got through those ten days without, as far as I was concerned, undue fatigue but with a real sense of peace.

That alone was remarkable, but what impressed me most was the extraordinary number of rapid and rather inexplicable recoveries that took place during those ten days. It was so noticeable that the staff remarked upon it though no one ever knew what was in my mind at the time. I had not myself expected it, rather the reverse, in view of the lack of normal medical procedures.

The experience was pin-pointed months after when one of the African nurses at the end of the morning round, asked me to go back and see one of my patients who was crying. When we asked her what was the matter, she said that she knew she would not get better because I had not 'touched her'. She said that people in her town who had recently been in hospital had returned home 'cured' saying it was because I had 'touched them'.

This I know can be explained away easily, but there remains the fact that in normal examinations, such as I had already performed on the patient in question, I had certainly touched a good deal. I think I always had a basic prayerful longing for each patient's recovery, but in the crisis described above there was obviously something else at work.[6]

• • •

Trying to capture the evidence of prayer on the world-wide stage to which we know it belongs is difficult; the stories, the experiences will diversify, but lose none of their significance in the telling.

Cecil Dobson, a retired headmaster, had a big decision to make. His wife Ann left it to him to decide if they should sell up and leave the house they had built over fifty years ago, and move, from Tynemouth, in the north of England, to Yorkshire, to be near their daughter and her family. Cecil worried and thought about it but could not make up his mind. He was, as he put it, 'fifty-fifty'. There was the wrench of leaving their friends, all the interests they had built up over the years, and of course their home – the home and the garden they had developed and nurtured from scratch. The trees were now at their best, the shrubs, everything had come to fruition, and now they were thinking about leaving it all behind. Cecil, always a religious man, could not decide, and so he 'finally and earnestly turned to prayer for an answer'. For two weeks he prayed, saying, 'Please help me; give me a sign, anything to help me in my decision.'

After the two weeks, he was at his church service as usual, and thrilled to have his answer; the minister read the passage from the Bible on God's call to Abraham; *'Get thee out of thy country'...*[7] Needless to say, Cecil and Ann did move to Yorkshire, and never regretted the decision.

A good old-fashioned example of the power of prayer comes from Devon, and it took place nearly one hundred years ago.

A vicar resided in a country parish in Devon with his huge family, and his great 'theme' was always 'prayer'. Everything had to be prayed about; the good times, the bad times, problems to be sorted, worries to be overcome. He would gather the whole family together in the largest sitting room in the house and 'take it to the Lord in prayer'. His long-suffering wife had indeed witnessed many wonders over the years, but now her patience was at an end as she faced the fact that the family, who were always poor, were now on the point of starvation. Having to rely on the kindness of parishioners was never easy, but this year had been especially hard for everyone, with near disastrous crops and poverty all around.

Trying to make her husband realise the seriousness of the situation, that they were now on to their last loaf of bread, she cringed when he answered in his usual, positive way, 'We will pray about it.'

Calmly gathering all the family together, as he began to lead the prayers, there was a knock at the door; on answering it, he found two liveried servants standing on the doorstep struggling to hold a huge hamper of food sent over by the Lord of the Manor.

The Lord had, on a whim (he was never to be found at his country seat at that particular time of year), returned unexpectedly to the country and, remembering the vicar and his family, immediately dispatched provisions, enough to last for months!

• • •

Of the endless stories of courage and self-sacrifice, faith, fear and foreboding, to come out of the First World War, the need to pray was often to be found 'centre stage'. And no more so than in the story of the young soldier, who, as they say, believed only in 'having a good time'. He had lived his young life to the full, drinking, gambling, and whatever else in the pursuit of pleasure – until he faced, along with thousands of other soldiers, almost certain death at the front line. As his turn neared to go 'over the top', terrified, he dropped to his knees in prayer. In a simple, automatic movement, but one made with an earnestness and sincerity he had never felt before, he begged God to save him, promising in return, to devote the rest of his life to serving others. Miraculously saved, he kept his promise, later becoming a much loved and respected vicar.

It was in the desert during the Second World War when Leslie Young found the need to pray. Leslie, from Nottingham, served with the Sherwood Rangers in the Army. He was in a tank crew – there were five of them – and as he says, the day that always stands out in his mind was when they were in the Halfaya Pass. It was 1942. He tells of feeling so 'bad and frightened and homesick, longing for my family', that he just fell to his knees in the sand, in front of everybody, asking the 'Good Lord' to get him through. He says that as the others looked on while he was praying, the Captain said, 'Say one for us.' Sadly he was the only one out of the group in the tank to survive.

When the German Field Marshall Rommel, known as 'The Desert Fox,' was captured, he said, 'I could have defeated your army, but I could not beat the power behind it.' By this he meant the power of prayer.

Suddenly, once again, in this our twenty-first century, it seems that 'spirituality' has become fashionable. Some years ago Oprah Winfrey said, 'I think there's a spiritual revolution about.' *Cosmopolitan*, the magazine of female emancipation, sexual equality and advice on how to get out of the kitchen and into a high powered job, has appointed 'a spirituality editor'.

Shelley von Strunckel, the astrologer of a *Sunday Times* magazine writes; '2004, the New Age, is finally becoming the Now Age. During this period, spiritual pursuits, philosophical studies and getting to know about one's inner world will gradually take over.'[8] And a magazine heading, 'Say A Little Prayer', describes disaffected, stressed-out young professional people searching for spiritual guidance to give their life new meaning; the article continued with another heading, 'There's More To Life Than Getting Wasted On A Friday Night'.

Another article, in the same magazine, reports the story of a young blonde executive, immaculately dressed, who works in a smart office in Soho. 'After a terrible day – her boss is in a foul temper, she has just had the row to end all rows with her boyfriend, and none of her friends has phoned her – she does something she would never have done five years ago. She closes her eyes and begins to pray.' Yet another young lady of thirty-five years who is a PR for Armani, admits to 'falling on her knees in prayer', when she 'really, really doesn't know the answer'. While a fashion stylist of thirty-three years who grew up with a Muslim father and a Christian mother says the concept of institutionalised religion is dated. Spirituality is about being connected, learning to be a good person, not obeying arcane rules or believing in one truth. Asked whom she says her twice-daily prayers to, she answers, 'I don't say them to a person, a god or goddess, but to a divine consciousness.'

Searching, seeking for spiritual guidance to give life new meaning – for something more than this world has to offer. The American author Neale Donald Walsch, whose book *Conversations with God* has been translated into twenty-seven languages, states: 'The world is starved for a new spiritual truth that could allow everyone to live in peace and harmony on this planet.' But it may not be a new spiritual truth we are looking for, simply a different interpretation of the old truth, with new emphasis on the spiritual side of our nature; bringing to the fore the spiritual, to achieve, as the Essenes strove to achieve, 'wholeness within'. Perhaps, from all we read and hear about today, there really is a turn, a return, to spirituality, to prayer, to a search for the true 'self'. Perhaps something unsavoury in our materialistic world has aroused an inner longing we need to assuage. Perhaps we have gone so far down the road of 'must have' and 'selfishness' that a U-turn is inevitable.

Whatever it is that is happening, a spiritual revolution or a gentle 'wake-up' call, there is obviously a need for reassurance of some sort; a need for a reason, a meaning for this existence of ours. And, in trying against all the odds, defying all the 'pulls', all the temptations of materialism to say 'enough is enough', and in looking for 'something more', we are taking the first important step towards the answer. We approach a truth which, in the final analysis, we will perhaps discover is to be found within.

Nancy Green, who lived in Glossop, Derbyshire, at the time, tells of a dreadful experience but one that proved to her the power of prayer.

> Old neighbours (I knew them as children and we had been friends for years) arrived to live next to me. They

were a young couple in their twenties. On January 8th, a very frosty morning, the husband, riding a bike in Stockport, had an accident. The police came and told his wife and asked her to go to the Stockport Infirmary at once. She asked me to go with her. When we got there, the doctor told us it was fatal and that he had been run over by a big Bleachers lorry in Wellington Road. His bike had skidded. Of course his wife went hysterical and had to be treated. I was asked to identify the body. Well I myself was suffering with shock and when I was taken to the mortuary, I was in a state of collapse, wondering what was facing me and how horrible it would be. Before I went through the door, I said a little prayer and asked God to help me. Immediately all fear left me, I stopped trembling and walked straight to where he was, and when they unveiled his face, there wasn't a blemish. I put my fingers through his wet hair and just said, 'Poor Stan.' The peace that was all around I shall never forget, I know it was an 'Act of God'.[9]

A kind and caring lady has often told me that when she makes a special, heart-felt plea in her prayers to help someone, anyone, there is always a response. Often it is not immediate, but her prayer never fails to be answered in one way or another; while a teacher in a school in South Africa vividly remembers talking to the children – aged nine years to twelve – in an assembly about prayer, and being surprised at their interest. A day or two after her talk one of the older boys excitedly told her he had tried 'this praying', and it worked! His dog had gone missing only days previously, but he was devastated and sick with worry. After he prayed about it, seemingly, to the boy, the dog 'just returned', out of the blue, and for him it was an answer to prayer.

Jean Hall, a popular and tireless worker for charity told everyone she was 'cushioned by prayer' after, having been ill with what she believed was a curable illness, she received the shattering news that she only had months to live. Once over the shock, her family decided they would live every day as if it was Christmas, and this they did, with Jean their strength and inspiration. How did she do it? Her simple answer; knowing there were so many prayers being said for her, and feeling so much love around her, she felt 'carried along', 'cushioned by prayer'.

Stan Miller, the husband of Sheila, a spiritual healer, both from Northumberland, did not believe in anything but he had always encouraged her in her work. After a serious illness overtook him, and as he was coming to the end of his life, he woke her at three a.m. one morning and asked if someone (possibly her friend Lilian who was also a healer) was giving him healing. He said he could feel hands on him. At eight that same morning Sheila phoned her friend, who assured her that she had indeed been sending him healing, and at that time.

Not a well person, Bell Lazenby was feeling ill on this particular day when her friend Gill phoned. Gill said she was going to the Catholic Church and would light a candle for her. A short time later Bell, not feeling any better, decided to go to bed. After about an hour, she seemed to take a turn for the worse, then amazingly a nun appeared, 'moving towards me at the foot of the bed towards the left. She carried a lighted candle. Suddenly, almost immediately, I recovered.'

Simple, everyday stories – a five-year-old girl in 1940 acutely ill with silent pneumonia, prayed over by her parents and Sunday school teacher, who 'pulled through', to astonishing stories of healing and miraculous cures when all hope was lost. Such incredible phenomena has prompted doctors and scientists all over the world to 'think again' about scientific facts and practices in medicine which were, until recent times, written in stone. To look again at the 'prayer factor', taking it to a new depth and with a rigour and seriousness perhaps neglected in the past. And, as one group of cardiologists in North Carolina, America, decided, to conduct a major experiment asking the question, from a scientific point of view, 'Does Prayer Work?'

One doctor/scientist who set up this ambitious project to test the 'power of prayer' explained, 'More and more people are asking people to pray for them and now science is trying to prove what everybody has known since people came out of the caves. That spirit is all around us. Can a person tap into it anytime? Yes. Is it possible for one person to heal another by praying?' And so they made a three-year study taking 750 heart patients, dividing them into two groups. Each patient had the same type of heart operation and it was life or death surgery. A computer was used to choose at random which of the two groups would be prayed for.

Within half an hour of the groups being chosen, prayer groups were notified which patients to pray for. Besides prayer groups in churches, e-mails were sent out to Buddhist monks in Tibet, to Jerusalem; to Muslims meeting in a carpet shop; Progressive Warriors meeting in an attic; ladies who meet for coffee and prayer. Groups from all over the world were united in prayer for six months of this experiment.

The results of the pilot study were astonishing. The patients who did best were all prayed for. The data results of the actual experiment are still being studied, but it appears on first conclusions of the basic data tables that prayer made no difference to the long-term health of patients, but music, images and touch seemed to help. Finally, the experiment continued by carrying out an extra trial whereby a second layer of prayer groups were created to pray for the first prayer groups. Having these extra groups did have a positive effect.

Comments and observations from the medical/science team were that: 'the human spirit also has a healing force. The human spirit guides the body as much as the body drives the spirit.' 'It is "natural" to "pray"; a clue to medicine that there *is* something. Prayer is connecting to that divine energy – the life force'. 'Surgeons and scientists are looking for a way we can help each other. They are fascinated with medicine and religion,' and 'We have underestimated the power of prayer in medicine. What else in the human being can help with illness?'

An interesting observation to come out of all this is, 'Was a factor in the experiment that the people praying for patients "did not know them personally?" ' (Yet 'absent' healing is popular and apparently successful.) With prayer, does that personal factor have to be there? Do you need to know the person you are praying for? Another point made was, 'Is it wise to put God to the test?', remembering Christ's warning to the Devil, 'Thou shalt not put thy God to the test.' But such a caution might well also apply to other forms of research into spiritual experiences.[10]

· · ·

> When I was twenty-one years, I was engaged to be married. At this time, my favourite grandma died. As she was dying, I was left with her while my aunt went for the doctor. The death rattle came into my grandma's throat and a huge fear gripped me. I went rigid and was petrified and raised my eyes to the heavens, when I heard a huge choir singing, 'Lead us Heavenly Father lead us'…the fear died in me, my aunt returned, and granny died.[11]

The lady, from Bolton, Lancashire, telling us of her great fear, describes perfectly what probably most people experience at least once in their lives, 'fear'. 'I went rigid and was petrified'; but whereas she raised her eyes to the heavens, from where she received her solace, the usual reaction appears to be to 'fall on our knees' in prayer; in total distress a sign of supplication, reverence, begging for help from a 'higher power'. Here a reminder of the words from an old hymn, 'For I have no help but Thee'.

A writer and investigator into the afterlife, who worked continuously, spending years writing and talking about his belief as a way of helping and comforting others, also emphasises the power of 'thought' in our lives.

> Remember, you don't have to go to church to pray. You don't even have to go down on your knees. Prayer is only another word for thought. Thought, intense and concentrated.[12]

It appears to be the depth of our thought, the intensity (usually manifesting when we are in greatest need) and, in praying for others, the sincerity and love – of the thought, 'intense and concentrated', that can move mountains.

Doris, a middle-aged lady from Texas, gives this account of her near-fatal accident as she was driving down a mountain and rounded a curve in the road.

> I looked up to see a fast travelling train coming out of the trees. Even though I wanted badly to slam on the brakes, I knew that there was no way to avoid hitting or being hit. So I screamed, 'What should I do?'

> A voice as clear as I have ever heard said, 'Put on the gas!' Going against my own will, I tried to beat the train – and I was hit at the back door of the car but never got knocked off the highway and came to a stop on the shoulder of the road.

As I opened my eyes, I believed surely I was about to meet my creator. But I felt surprise, then disappointment, then happiness (to see that I was alive and unhurt).

Nearby workers said that if I had put on the brakes, the train would have hit me broadside and dragged the car far down the tracks.[13]

There are essentially two kinds of prayer – intense and concentrated prayer from an individual or, as in mass prayers at Holy Shrines such as Lourdes in France, where, it is believed, through the immense power generated, a divine intervention takes place and miraculous cures are witnessed.

In the Andean jungle near Cuzco in Peru, in 1998, a huge fire was started by lightening. There was no way of saving the temples of Machu Pichu. Everything was tried, but the weather pattern was not going to change and the sacred temples were doomed; that is, until the exhausted natives decided to go back to the old ways of doing things when help or advice was needed. They started to pray.

Within a few hours the impossible took place. A low-pressure system developed over Machu Pichu and a mass of moist warm air from the coast merged with the cold dry air of the mountains. Rain fell down on Machu Pichu in torrents and wiped out a fire that, before prayer time, the people had given up all hope of ever putting out. The rescue was so impressive that even government officials were mystified. But for the villagers there was no mystery, only a thankfulness that their prayers had worked again.[14]

Prayer can also be the bearer of a communication with a premonition:

While praying at bedtime, I had a strong visual

assurance. A car going around a sharp right-hand curve crashed end over end off an embankment.

Then, the palm of a hand was raised in front of me, as if in a warning to stop.

Several months later, I was in an accident where a young man died. The happening (including my stopping at the right moment) was exactly as in the vision.[15]

And it is, understandably, often during a quiet time of prayer when mystical experiences that completely change lives happen.

One night when I was saying my prayers I suddenly felt a great light all around me and I seemed to be walking or rather floating up between rows of figures towards something of intense brightness, and a voice said, 'Go your way in peace and your ways shall be shown unto you.'

But the light was like nothing on earth, it was all around and uplifted me with an indescribable feeling.

Since that day I have not worried about any decision I may have to make, as I know that the way that has opened for me has been the right one and always will be.[16]

A 1980-81 survey in Gallop Poll showed that nearly one-third of all Americans – about forty-seven million people – have had what they call a religious or mystical experience. Of this group fifteen million report an otherworldly feeling of union with a divine being. They describe such things as special communications from deceased people or divine beings, visions of unusual lights, and out-of-body experiences.

> I was reading the Bible one night and couldn't sleep. A vision appeared to me. I was frozen and motionless. I saw an unusual light that wasn't there – but was. There was a great awareness of someone else being in that room with me.

In another case, a young man felt a deep sense of God's presence late one night just before he went to bed. After he climbed into bed, the sense of the supernatural continued to be so intense that his body seemed to become weightless and to rise slightly off his bed.[17]

The fact that people seem to change after a prayer, or out-of-body experience, or healing, or some other form of mystical experience, proves to us that such experiences cannot be simply classified, for each is totally unique and personal. Linda Sharp from Devon shares an experience that happened to her when she was twenty-two years, and proved to her the reality of God and the power of prayer.

> Alone in my room, feeling extremely desperate about the seeming foolishness of life, I asked, out loud, that 'If there is a God, could He help?' I was immediately overwhelmed by the feeling of a Presence/Light/ Love, all around; it seemed everywhere, I really can't explain. It appeared to last for a minute or two, although I can't be sure. I lost all sense of time. I was left with an indescribable feeling of peace and joy.
>
> This moment completely changed my life. Everything suddenly seemed to make sense. Now, years later, I still

look back to those few moments as the most real and important in my life. I am firmly convinced in the reality of God (called by whatever name) and the power of prayer. I have an inner certainty that life, even under the most tragic circumstances, is good. Even more so now than in childhood, I feel a great love for the world and everyone in it.[18]

Another lady tells us that many years ago she had a very painful and frightening experience to go through.

Thank God, I had always believed in prayer and knelt to pray for what must have been two hours.

There were tears everywhere; I felt weak and so alone. Then I truly felt a brightness around me and a firm hand on my shoulder; words just can't explain it, but I knew I was not alone. Afterwards nothing had changed. I still had the ordeal to go through, but not alone. I came through it a better person because of it.[19]

The experience of 'being born again' happened to Moira when she was thirty-two years, and she can never forget and still marvels at the change that took place within her, and, as she says, 'the gracious way in which it was carried out'.

Although I had what is called a nervous breakdown, I knew also that it was a breakdown in human relationships. Not being able to go to church, I continued in prayer at home and gradually all the things I had learned in Sunday school and church became clearer in meaning.

As I prayed, I realised I was being made to think, and that thought made me change personally – from being a self-conscious and uncertain person to one of peace and certainty. Becoming sensitive to the needs of others and less sensitive in myself, and not taking offence easily.[20]

• • •

Once again it was at the time of the First World War when John Patterson found strength and revelation through prayer. He was twenty-three years old at the time.

I was called up to serve in the First World War, but by then I was an uncompromising pacifist, the only one of my family. I was sent first to an NCC unit and then court-martialled for refusing to obey orders and sentenced to two years in prison.

My cell was on the ground floor of one hall. The first fourteen nights I had to sleep on the board bed without a mattress and did not sleep well at all. Moreover, I began to suffer from claustrophobia badly. One night a younger man in the next cell to me – a young Quaker – cracked up badly.

His screams caused a commotion and he was taken away. Then it was my turn and I was first on the point of breaking up likewise when the situation changed dramatically.

I was praying then and, I think, sobbing too – quietly – when the prison 'vanished'. I was looking up at the stars. And at one star in particular, the light of which shot up and outward to form a complete cross. It seemed to say to me, 'By this Sign, Conquer!'

I rolled onto a very sore hip and went off to sleep. Next morning and always thereafter I was utterly happy. Nothing could affect me!

Warders commanded me to 'Take that smile off your face'! Had no effect whatever. My smile was permanent. When one officer on the exercise yard ordered 'Double march', I ran and ran, with a broken shoe on one foot until everyone else had given in and dropped out! And I was never a runner!

From that night I have never doubted the reality of God as some 'one', not an 'it' – not an ultimate reality or principle but someone who was near. Now at seventy-seven plus, He still is!

I quoted at a Quaker meeting the saying of a Jewish Rabbi, 'Three factors are necessary to make a life significant. They are God, a Soul and a moment.' I added, when quoting these words, 'The three are always present, but the recognition not always. The moment is just the moment of recognition. And that may be one or one half of a second, but it will illuminate a whole lifetime and never end. That is the Eternal Now which a man, a woman or a child may experience once and for all time. I did and I know it![21]

The moment of recognition is the moment of truth. As mentioned in an earlier chapter, so many people, listening and talking about the experiences of others call out, 'Why doesn't this happen to me? Why have I not had such and such an experience?' But perhaps they *have*. Perhaps they have had an inkling of 'something'; 'not dared to delve into, or make time for, or cared enough about it to make time for'. Perhaps the something came in a dream; a sudden premonition; a surge of feeling, of elation, of love; in a sense of 'knowing'; in a previously unbelievable unimagined situation; or in despair.

'the moment is fleeting' –

'the whole thing probably didn't last longer than a second or two'

'of course, seconds later I hadn't the faintest idea what it was all about'

'we must have passed this spot in a matter of seconds but it seemed like minutes'

'the feeling doesn't stay with you, it's only there for a second or so, but you're given the strength and knowledge to carry on'

'it lasted about half a minute and was like nothing else I have ever experienced'

'suddenly there was a blinding flash of light – after a few moments the vision and the brightness left me'

'in the twinkling of an eye, my consciousness was raised to the full awareness of the fourth dimension of the mind, the 'Kingdom of the Heavens'. I realised there was a whole new, unexplored world lying just beyond this veil of our senses'

'just a passing glance and it was gone'

A passing glance, but a moment that if captured can 'illuminate a whole lifetime' and *never* end. A moment when we 'know' something we did not know. When a thought, an emotion, an experience, triggers off an affinity – an all-embracing timeless, space-less, reality with the 'unnamed something', the 'universal energy', the 'life force', 'God'. But the moment is fleeting; just a passing glance, and it is gone.

A little red prayer box was mentioned at the beginning of this chapter, with scrolls/prayers to pick out at random for advice or comfort in times of trouble. It may be, however, that we don't need a prayer box or any other device to help us in our search, our need. For questioning leads to searching, searching leads to answers and, in the words of a Catholic Priest, 'A struggle for anything will not go unrewarded.'

Answers seem to be there, all around us, all the time, when we become 'aware'. When she is feeling 'down', a lady called Mrs Robinson from Sussex claims she never fails to be helped by hearing the song played on the radio: 'And as for you, Mrs Robinson, Jesus loves you more than you can know.' And she says this happens just as she tunes in, at home, in the car, or wherever.

A massive billboard by the side of a main road near Edinburgh has the heading, 'MIRACLES, HEALING, FAITH', with a picture of a healer and information on meetings; while an ecumenical church on the outskirts of another city seems to bring no end of comfort and answers to countless people who pass by. The words on the billboard, presented in huge bold print, are easy to read, often changed, yet still apply to most situations. 'You are not alone; Let Go Let God'; while the latest one, with the first line in colour and the second line printed in strong capital letters, reads dramatically;

> If you do not believe in God
> YOU HAD BETTER BE RIGHT.

(A more traditional form of prayer would be, 'The world is sustained by the prayers of the Righteous', and 'Prayer is the longing of the soul'.)

We are presented with words of wisdom (help) in so many ways. It could be the sudden recalling of a memory that confronts us; a casual conversation, a sentence in a magazine or newspaper (a man's whole life was changed by a newspaper he found lying on a seat in a London bus). A telephone call; missing our usual train or bus can have amazing repercussions; an unexpected visit, a surprise meeting. Life carries us along, and we rarely know the 'depth', or the 'hidden' outcome of events.

In the hurly-burly of our journey here, passing through the many doorways of experience, finding ourselves part of undreamed-of scenes, vistas, often living as if stepping (or being 'thrust'), onto a stage; sometimes the main character, sometimes the 'bit' player. Whatever, and always, recognised or not recognised, it appears to be that we carry within us our inheritance. A deep-seated, inner knowledge; an inherent understanding of a guiding force of love – ours for the taking on the moment of recognition, and reached through a power which knows no bounds; the power of prayer.

For some it will be a power to adhere to from time to time:

> I was under such pressure and carrying such a weight of sadness that I didn't know what to do, which way to turn. Someone, seeing my despair and not knowing how to advise me said, 'Why don't you just leave it all in God's hands?' I did and felt immediate relief.

When I get into real difficulties, and I do, it's prayer to God that solves these things.

To many, prayer will be the bedrock of their lives:

I am a great believer in prayer. I have often had doubts, but something soon happens to eliminate that. I have had so many answers that I couldn't count them all, but I never ask for anything frivolous. In any difficulty I ask and I receive. Last year I could hardly walk. Now I walk normally. I've lost important things in the home and failed to find them. I ask and they turn up.

I have a bed-sitter and had trouble with insects in my bed, such as an earwig or small beetle. I asked and since have seen none. I had a little trouble with an electric gadget one day. I asked for help and a knock came to the door. A friend had unexpectedly called and soon put matters to right. You will know what this means when I tell you that I am over eighty years old and live alone. I ask for sleep when going to bed and I get eight hours almost every night. I am rather nervous, so I ask for help and a deep peace comes upon me. I prayed hard for a friend who was very ill. She recovered and the doctor said it was a miracle.

These are only a few of the things that have happened to me, as I have been helped all my life. If I get no reply, I accept it as a part of God's wisdom. We do not give our own children everything they ask for. I have been helped in big things, too, but small things are important, as they prove your trust in God.[22]

Rahimullah, in his sixties, lives with his family in Afghanistan where he tends the British Cemetery in Kabul. His prayers are all important to him. He prays five times a day, waking up with the first call to prayer at three-thirty or four a.m.

> When I pray I feel light, and I always want to smile when
> I finish. If you don't pray you feel heavy.[23]

There are those who turn to prayer from time to time; those for whom prayer is a bedrock, and there will always be those who lead by example:

He was a good and well loved man, fifty-seven years old, facing the end of his life after a long, severe illness, the way he had always lived it, with patience and courage.

One day as he sat in his chair, deep in thought, his wife gently asked him, 'What are you doing, what are you thinking, when you sit there so quiet, not saying anything for such a long time?'

He answered, 'I'm praying.'

Choked with emotion, and recalling all the loving things she wanted to say to him, and all the unanswered questions she wanted to ask him, she simply replied, 'That's nice.'

• • •

True to say, we are what we are and we go where we go, but apparently, we will all, eventually, no matter how long it takes, find 'that' moment:

> in the twinkling of an eye, my consciousness was raised
> to the full awareness of the fourth dimension of the
> mind, the 'Kingdom of the Heavens'. I realised there
> was a whole new, unexplored world lying just beyond
> this veil of our senses.

and in reading about the experiences of others, we may discover that we ourselves have been helped over a hurdle; perhaps to find that moment of recognition (which inevitably translates into the moment of truth); perhaps to take the first step towards a 'something' that, given the chance, can become 'everything' in our lives – can become everything, and never let us down.

Chapter Five

God's Magic

'All embracing; running through every beat of life, every circumstance, both in nature and in human kind; in the seen and unseen worlds; often unnoticed.'

PARANORMAL EXPERIENCES ARE ALMOST impossible to classify. Unique and personal, they overlap one into another and range from the unbelievable to a simple straightforward case of intuition. But whatever the experience, that element of magic, always present, touches the recipient in some strange way, opening previously closed and uninterested minds to amazing possibilities. The magic of 'impulse', 'intuition', has probably happened to most of us at some time in our lives, and was certainly an eye opener for Alan who had never experienced anything like it before.

• • •

While driving home from work on the motorway a few years ago, Alan Bell had a sudden unexplainable urge to visit his mother who was ill in a nearby hospital. Yet why should he do this, as it was already arranged that he would visit her within the next few hours with his wife Joan? A steady, salt of the earth type of man, practical by nature and not given to fanciful ideas, Alan, completely out of character, fortunately acted on his impulse. A few hours later would have been too late.

• • •

The dictionary defines intuition as: 'power of knowing without reasoning or being taught'. Could we perhaps add to that? – 'intuition': an extra sensory perception; another way in which the 'unnamed something', the 'universal energy', the 'life-force', 'God', communicates with us. Is the sense we call 'intuition' *direct illumination from the Divine Mind'?*[1]

Air Chief Marshal Lord Dowding, commander in chief of fighter command, a position he held from 1936 to 1940, coined the phrase 'God's Magic', and used it as the title for a book in which he explains the importance of the intuition (sometimes called the sixth sense) as:

> a coupling-up of the mind to the Universal Intelligence so that we may reach the shores of 'knowledge which lie deeply hidden in the subconscious of every human being, so that true inspiration may be always available at need.

He advises: 'What the reason cannot accept, think over well. What the intuitive power cannot accept, reject.'[2]

• • •

Science has moved forward in its thinking with regard to our 'sixth sense'. An article in *The Times*, June 2004, with the heading 'Didn't you know it; there is sixth sense', reports that researchers have been surprised by experiments which suggest humans could have paranormal powers. More restrained commentators point out that a vast amount of so-called evidence into the paranormal has failed to convince most scientists, or most people, that a sixth sense exists. Emma King, however, who runs classes for developing the sixth sense in Glasgow and Edinburgh, believes that by training the sense our lives would be improved. 'Everybody has the ability, but some people have more than others.' She continues, 'We had more of a sixth sense thousands of years ago but that has been lost because of the way society works today.'

A lecturer in positive psychology at Cambridge University, Dr Nick Baylis urges us not to disregard our intuition. He refers to the growing number of experimenters in this field and reports that 'premonition' served 'another promising arena', explaining that in 1995, Congress and the CIA asked statistician Jessica Utts to evaluate American government studies into paranormal phenomena. Part of her 'unequivocally positive conclusions' stated that 'recent experiments suggest that if there is a psychic sense, then it works much like our other five senses and scans the future for major change, much as our eyes scan the environment for visual change'.[3]

There are many instances of doctors being led 'by a greater power' to the right action. One doctor expressed this as being led by intuition, and at another time being influenced by the figure of the Virgin Mary. He tells how at the age of twenty-seven, he intuitively knew how to remove a diphtheritic membrane from a child's throat, and on another occasion how he was influenced by a figure of the Virgin Mary to operate on a 'hopeless obstetric case', which was successful.[4]

In 1947, another doctor, who describes himself as non-religious, was tempted to give up his exacting job in his first senior post in charge of an accident unit. Suddenly, an inner voice said, 'This is the work you have always wanted to do. You wished to help others and now is your chance to fulfil your destiny that you wanted.' This had the effect of encouraging him to continue, and he could remember the exact spot where it happened, but he never again had a similar experience.[5]

The animal kingdom, nature, abounds with examples of 'motivation from a greater power', sharing with us the wonder of intuition, premonition, and in what can only be termed as 'God's Magic', know our thoughts and sense our feelings. Animals have been proved to be psychic.

Tigger was a fierce, wild, tortoiseshell cat. Fluffy and bonny, he turned up one day in Joyce and Eddies' garden; animal lovers who fed and cared for him as much as he would allow, and who spent months trying to coax him into their home before winter set in. Gradually they won him over, but still only on his terms – he always kept his distance from both them and the other member of the family, Blackie the cat (who, incidentally, ignored him). Over the years, Eddie had to wear strong gardening gloves if he needed to handle Tigger. Taking him to the vet, along with Blackie, for injections and so on, was a major operation needing perfect skill and timing. Never, but never, would Tigger voluntarily come close, until, one day, a good friend and neighbour, not visibly showing signs of distress, but inwardly in a state of turmoil, called. Hardly had she sat down to talk and seek advice from Joyce and Eddie when Tigger jumped onto her knee, cuddling into her while at the same time staring straight into her face with an unmistakable show of love and concern. For one moment, all life in that home was suspended. In complete amazement, three adults focused their whole attention on Tigger.

Eileen who lives in Scotland, loves all animals, but especially dogs. In 2001, she writes, her older dog was seriously ill, and the heartbreak when it died was almost unbearable. One day, in all her misery, she suddenly felt uplifted, a peace, a loving warm feeling engulf her, and although she didn't see him, she knew her dog was there with her, willing her not to be sad. She told her husband of this feeling but stressed it was more than a feeling – it was a knowledge, a certainty, that the dog still lived and would continue to be in their lives.

'Willing her not to be sad'; sharing our thoughts and feelings, helping us in strange, mysterious ways, in magical ways, as in the story of the psychic seagull.

Rachel Flynn, eighty-two, from Cape Cod, America, was out walking alone, when she fell over a thirty-foot cliff onto a lonely beach. After the accident, Rachel was too badly hurt to move, and believed she would remain there until she passed.

As she lay trapped between large boulders, a seagull hovered over her. Rachel wondered if it could be Nancy, one of those she and her sister fed at their home and knew so well that they gave them names.

The injured woman called out, 'For God's sake, Nancy, get help.'

Flying off to the house Rachel shared with her sister June, the bird tapped on the kitchen window, flapping its wings and 'making more noise than a wild turkey', June commented.

She tried to shoo it away, but the bird persisted. After fifteen minutes, June decided it might be trying to tell her something. When the bird flew ahead, stopping occasionally and looking back, June followed it. When it alighted at the cliff edge, June looked over – and saw her trapped sister.

The fire brigade was called and Rachel, taken to hospital, was found to be suffering from a badly twisted knee and severe bruising.[6]

How did that wild bird know someone was in distress, how did it know how to summon assistance?

That humans are not the only partakers of 'God's magic' is apparent; that animals possess strange and unexplained powers has been generally accepted for thousands of years. How could they perform the most unbelievable feats of courage and loyalty, travelling thousands of miles over deserts, mountains, the most hazardous of territory to reach home, if they were not guided by 'a greater power'. And the magical feeling of peace and love, expressed by Eileen, that came as she suddenly 'knew' her dog who had died – still lived, and was 'willing her not to be sad', comes in many different ways.

Joan Husband, an amateur artist, determined to honour a very special little Yorkshire Terrier, Toby. Toby unstintingly helped Joan to look after his owner, her mother, during a sad time of illness, and she decided, a few years after he passed, to try and paint his likeness from a photograph. One day, as she worked on the picture, she instinctively turned and noticed, set on the edge of his grave (which is in the corner of what is a fairly large garden), a tiny cluster of forget-me-nots. This was in the month of October, and they stayed well into winter, defying frost and all inclement weather to shine out in a beautiful hue of blue; and this in a garden of shrubs and trees with no such flower. Visitors, seeing the forget-me-nots, tried to explain them away with comments such as 'the wind or the birds will have dropped the seeds'. But why would they have been dropped right on Toby's grave, with a large garden to choose from, and appear in the month of October, and at the very time Joan was painting his picture?

Strange, but true, as is another story, the story of a coin.

Missing her husband to the point of despair, Sylvia Walton was only able to pick up the pieces of her life through her firm belief that he was still with her, simply in another dimension. Almost three years after his passing, she continued talking to him and seeking his advice, and was sensitive to any means he might use to contact her.

One day, wandering around a huge shopping mall with its thousands of visitors every day (known as the biggest shopping mall in Europe), and reminiscing on how they had enjoyed such strolls together, Sylvia sent out the plea, 'You *are* still with me aren't you? You haven't really gone, you do hear me,' and then chastised herself for doubting as she had received so much evidence of his continued existence. Then, even more disappointed in herself at her weak belief, still strolling around the mall, she asked him, in thought, if he really was there, to do something to prove his presence.

Having purchased an item in one of the stores, instead of putting the change away in her purse immediately as she usually did (she rarely checked it), she held it in her hand until she reached the door leading into the precinct. Not knowing 'why' at the time, she opened her hand to look at it and gasped in shock as there, shining out amidst all the other coins, was a tiny gold one, embossed with a palm tree. And she clearly saw (although she needs reading glasses for small print) the name Bahrain set around the edge. All this in the not-so-good lighting of a shopping mall. 'Bahrain was where they had lived out some of their happiest memories. Her husband had worked in Saudi Arabia for nineteen years and Sylvia was a regular visitor.'

In similar vein, flowers play a major part in the next experience, an experience that, as Sarah Clark tells us, showed how God's magic touched her life.

It was almost two weeks to Valentine's Day, February 14th 2002, and already I was dreading the time and longing for it to be over. My husband John had died in December 2001 and this was to be my first Valentine's Day without him for many years; a celebration we had kept together for the love, the romanticism, and the fun.

And so I started sending thoughts out to my so-called 'departed husband', asking if he would try and arrange for something nice, something 'special', to happen on that day. If something nice, or 'special' happened, I promised that I would accept it without doubt, as being from him. A tall order I know, but I was insistent in my thoughts. No one else knew of this.

A close friend Cath, was in Jamaica for a two-week holiday with her cousin. She couldn't explain it, but she had a strong urge to bring back for me, as a present, a box of 'Birds of Paradise' flowers, despite her cousin scoffing, 'You don't take flowers for another woman.'

After the two weeks, they left Jamaica very early on Mon. 11th Feb. to be home by Tues. 12th. but the plane, after three hours into the journey, had to return to Jamaica because of a technical fault. They finally arrived home on Wednesday 13th Feb.

Immediately on her arrival home, she phoned me, concerned that the flowers had been cramped in a box since the Monday, tossed around, on and off planes – but I was not at home. Failing to contact me until the evening (when I was already showered and ready for bed), we decided to leave the flowers, which she told me about, as long as they were in a cool place, until the next morning when I would collect them.

It was not until later that same night when, incredulous, I realised the significance of the present. Remembering my request to my husband to try and do something special for me on Valentine's day – and stressing that I would not doubt it was from him – here, now, on the very day, a box of flowers, from Jamaica.

It was not until months later, hearing the story, another

friend pointed out, 'Birds of Paradise'; 'Flowers from heaven'. A double whammy!

God's Magic, making the ordinary stories of life special; turning the ordinary stories of life into the extraordinary, the seemingly 'far fetched', unbelievable; through some infallible ingredient, some fleeting intervention. Through an omnipresence that runs through all things, sometimes unnoticed; perhaps unrecognised; often unaccepted.

Ken Sadler was eleven years old when he first saw her. A little fair-haired girl he picked out in a crowd at school and, strange as it may seem, immediately knew that he loved her. Meeting up with her one day on a walk (she was with other girls), he was so struck by her that he just had to go over and give her a kiss. She just smiled, but he was wild with joy and ran home with feet not touching the ground.

Not long after, he was devastated to find she had been sent home – she was an evacuee from London – and no one knew where she lived. He asked around but there was no one who knew anything about her life away from the village.

Years passed, but he never forgot the girl, Beryl. He could not get over his feelings, his first love. Even when he married, happily, it was still Beryl he thought of and wondered where she was. He had three sons, and over the years, mentioned to his wife about the little girl Beryl. She didn't mind him contacting agencies to try and trace her, but no luck.

Now, over fifty years had passed; his sons grown up, and his wife ill with cancer. As she deteriorated, finally, she was in and out of comas, only coming round for a matter of moments; but just before she passed, to his amazement, she said to him, 'Persevere. She's a long way away but you *will* find her.' He couldn't get his wife's words out of his head. How did she know?!

After her death, he continued the search, and finally found Beryl in Australia. At last, after nearly sixty years, they were married.[7]

An elderly lady writes of a memory she has from when she was a young child; a memory of an experience that, as she says, has never left her, and has always comforted her.

> As a young child, no more than three, I had to be taken away from my mother to stay with relatives in the north of Scotland. I remember sobbing in my little bed and no one coming to me. Then, I heard the local church bells chime, and they were ringing part of a refrain, a lullaby my mother used to sing to me. I listened, then fell into a deep, soothing sleep.[8]

It was during the miners' strike of 1984 when the next incident occurred, an incident that, in looking back, has the stamp of a bit of magic in it, for the recipient.

George Jones, a miner, and a staunch supporter of the miners strike, always a 'giver' rather than a 'taker', was finding life difficult money-wise. It was the birthday of his wife Norah, and again, Norah was a person who didn't look for anything for herself, and gave no thought to the fact that there would be no birthday present for her this year. As long as the family were looked after.

On this day, George was digging in the back garden, seeing to his vegetables, and he had just laid a bale of manure on the patch when his eye caught something glinting in the soil. He picked it up and took it indoors. Norah watched as, fully engrossed, he seemed to be washing a tiny object under the tap. Finally turning to her, he simply said, 'Here's your birthday present,' and with that gave her what turned out to be a most beautiful, solid silver, antique ring.

· · ·

So much 'magic' happening in ordinary, daily life. Could it be perhaps an inner desire that is met; the way we 'think', the way we live; an in-built concern for others; a (though maybe mainly unrecognised) 'natural' sending out of good, caring 'vibes' that attracts the special 'something'.

Harold Sharp was a well-known healer, writer, philosopher; one of those people you count a great privilege to have known. In the mid-sixties, he retired to his newly built bungalow on the outskirts of London and looked forward to a quiet retirement tending his herb garden and entertaining his many visitors. There were other bungalows in various stages of development around his, but the one opposite had the gentleman and his wife living there, although it was still in the final stages of completion.

Trying to have a friendly word or two with the gentleman as he worked around his bungalow, Harold was always rebuffed with an unpleasant, almost grumpy, reply. The man's unpleasantness upset him, and tended to put a blight on the atmosphere of the place. And it saddened Harold to think of someone being so obviously unhappy; but what could he do about it? The man was determined to have nothing to do with him.

One night, just before he retired to bed, Harold stood, as he usually did, with curtains pulled back, gazing admiringly through his large picture window at what was to him, the miracle of the night sky. There, stretching out endlessly before him, in all its splendour, was the beauty of creation – velvet sombre clouds hosting a luminous saucer moon, accompanied by sparkling dots for stars; blending together, displaying the harmony of the heavens. He couldn't suppress a heartfelt cry at the perfection of it all; then, thinking deeply and sadly about the unpleasant situation that was around him, in his thoughts he cried out, 'Oh why can't we have such peace, such harmony here, here on the earth plane?'

The next morning, Harold noticed his grumpy neighbour busy outside as usual but, not as usual, it was the neighbour who shouted over to Harold to come and have coffee and taste some home-cooking with himself and his wife.

So started a sincere and lasting friendship between the three of them; but Harold, despite all the marvellous things he had both witnessed and experienced during his long life, never failed to be impressed by the way in which it had all been brought about.

Harold gazed admiringly at the miracle of the night sky, seeing it in all its beauty and perfection, but Hazel tells how she *heard* the music of the spheres and how the sheer grandeur and simplicity of it all filled her with amazement and delight.

> The experience I am relating here took place in the summer. I had spent the weekend with friends and because of a sudden train strike I had to return by bus which deposited me half a mile from my home in the middle of the night: it could have been 1.30 a.m. I began to walk across the common. It was quite dark of course – street lamps had all been switched off, and there was no traffic – but the night was warm and still, and the sky full of stars. I had no particular feeling beyond a slight nervousness about being out so late in a lonely spot; on the whole I think I was enjoying the walk.

> I had nearly reached my mother's house when I suddenly realised that the whole sky was alive with sound. Out of the deep silence grew a whole orchestration – not of music, but of a harmonious blending of sounds, as though an infinite number of radio transmitters were emitting signals, each one with its own unique pitch and rhythm of pulsation. There

was no melody and no form: I just knew that what I was hearing was the music of the spheres, something that has no beginning and no ending, and the grandeur and simplicity of this filled me with amazement and delight. At the same time I vividly recalled the taste of painted metal and my memory tugged me straight back to the nursery in another house, where, night after night (though I had totally forgotten it until that moment) I had stood as a tiny child, sucking the bars at the window and listening to the stars.

I arrived at my mother's house and went indoors; upstairs in my bedroom I could still hear the stars singing, and they continued to do so until I reluctantly went to sleep. I have never heard this sound again, though I have often longed to do so for the joy and satisfaction it brought. Perhaps the oddest part of this experience was that it felt so normal.

Soon afterwards I began working on an army training film dealing with radio relay, and I took the opportunity of questioning the officer acting as adviser. He assured me that stars do in fact emit radio signals, and he explained patiently and at length why human ears are unable to receive these signals. I did not tell him of my experience – but I have shared it with friends from time to time, and one close friend told me that he had had a very similar experience late one night while serving as a naval officer in the Red Sea.[9]

As in the story of the man who found a silver ring in the garden, concerned at not having the money to buy a birthday present for his wife, could it really be possible that a 'natural', sincere, sending out of good vibes attracts the 'special something'? Diana Thompson seems to think so.

I was thirty-five years old at the time and the mother of four children. We lived next to a somewhat crotchety old man, who lived on his own. Whenever we went on holiday, he insisted on having the key of our house 'so that he could keep an eye on things'. As soon as we returned from holiday, he would appear immediately to give us a blow-by-blow account of what had been happening to him in our absence. As you may imagine, this was not always welcome in the throes of unpacking, seeing to the children, etc.!

However, on this particular holiday, he was thwarted, as we did not arrive home until 11 p.m. I fully expected him to appear early the next morning. But 9 a.m. 10 and 11 came and went, and there was still no sign of him. At midday I was in the kitchen, cleaning out the refrigerator, which was full of green mould! I said casually to my husband, 'You'd better look in to see how old C is.' A few minutes later I heard them chatting and laughing in the street outside. 'Good, he's all right then,' I thought with relief.

As I said these words to myself, the kitchen and garden were filled with golden light. I became conscious that at the centre of the Universe, and in my garden, was a great pulsing dynamo that ceaselessly poured out love. This love poured over and through me, and I was part of it and it wholly encompassed me. 'Perfectly me, I was perfectly part of perfection.'

The vision was gone in a moment, leaving me with a strong desire to rush out and embrace anyone I could find, including Mr C. It was overwhelmingly real, more real than anything I had ever experienced, even though I had been in love, and the feelings after the birth of each of my children had been wonderful. The vision was of a far 'realer' quality. To deny it would be the ultimate sin, the blasphemy.

Meditating upon the event, I think the fact that it happened when for once in my life I was altruistically *concerned for the well-being of another person* is significant. I may also say that I had never before read anything about mystical experience – although I did afterwards, of course.

I wish I could say that I became a miraculously saintly being afterwards. On the contrary, I have gone through a long period of psychological trauma, having to face some hard truths about myself! It is rather as if I had been taken to the top of the mountain, shown a marvellous land, and then been taken to the bottom of the mountain and been told I must climb to the top if I wish to dwell in the land which I now know exists. I have no excuse now for un-loving behaviour towards another – a gift of grace brings awesome responsibility'![10]

The magic, the gift, known as the 'power of thought', is no mean responsibility, especially when we stop to consider what could be the consequences, if wrongly applied.

Penny Milburn, a pleasant and hard-working head of department in a large inner city comprehensive school, could not understand why, apparently, she was the only member of staff unable to 'get on' with Bill, another head of department. Bill was hugely popular with both staff and pupils and an expert in his field; they hadn't had any disagreements and their work was not closely linked, but with Penny, there was always an uncomfortable feeling in Bill's presence, and a sensitivity of sarcasm whenever (which was not often), he spoke to her.

Surprised at her feelings – this situation was unusual for her – Penny, in a roundabout way, quizzed other members of staff about Bill and found them all to be of the same opinion; he was a 'regular, sincere, cheerful and helpful guy'.

Now, with a new timetable, she found herself the only other person in the staff room with Bill, their so-called 'free time' coinciding, and, in Penny's mind anyway, the situation seemed to deteriorate dramatically. While Bill could joke and pass the time of day, on the friendliest of terms, with anyone who might pop into the staff room, not one word passed between the two of them. The discomfort felt by Penny intensified. Giving the situation more consideration than perhaps it deserved, analysing it over and over again in her mind, Penny decided to put the 'power of thought', which she already knew something about, to the test.

Was she the one putting barriers up between them she wondered? Was it her own poor attitude towards Bill that caused the tension? And her answer had to be an honest 'yes'. For whatever reason, and she hadn't yet worked that out, she realised that she herself must have created the situation with her negative attitude, and on acknowledging this, immediately put into practice 'right thinking'.

Penny started sending out strong, positive, sincere friendly thoughts to Bill, asking for the situation between them to change; and it did. Almost immediately! So soon was the change put into operation that she was startled and unbelieving at first.

Bouncing into the staff room in his usual way, beaming, and seeing only Penny sitting there, instead of ignoring her, Bill called across excitedly, 'Hey Penny…'

And now, all barriers down, there were two outcomes to this little test; one, the start of a happy and lasting working relationship; and two, the indisputable proof for Penny of the 'power of thought'.

Thoughts to help with relationships, and thoughts that, if we take time quietly to ponder on them, then we will be given wise direction on this often difficult pathway of ours; such as the advice given by the author Joseph F Girzone in his book *Never Alone*.

> Do not allow yourself to take offence when someone inflicts injury upon you. Understand the anguish and the pressures in their life and the pain that prompted their thoughtless or warped behaviour, then you will pity them and keep at bay pain and grief you would have suffered had you allowed the offence to take hold of you.

> In this way you will stay free and uncluttered with anger and resentment. I tell you this as the key to true inner peace.

True self-awareness, or a sudden realisation that we are more than the physical body we inhabit, is the magic that happened to Ann Dickie, a professional dancer; but as usual, she had to discover this the hard way.

Dancers have to cope with a lot of injuries and, as Ann tells us, she was only sixteen when she felt the first twinges of something that led, when she was in her mid-forties, to her having a double hip replacement. It was, she believed, the end of her dancing career.

Suffering much pain, and learning how to conceal it – dancers have to remember that no one is going to employ a dancer who is not fit – Ann can hardly believe how she got through the years. She remembers once in her early thirties being in Scotland with Ballet Rambert and ending up in casualty, the pain becoming so unbearable. Yet somehow she kept going. She taught the degree course at Surrey University and directed the National Youth Dance Company; but says she knew she was going downhill fast.

Not very practical, Ann tells us; 'Dancers often aren't, I never imagined I'd clap out. I hadn't put money aside or bought my own flat. I was on my own, two flights up, in a council bed-sit. What was most depressing was the isolation. There were some dodgy people around.'

Ann describes gritting her teeth and how she had to psyche herself up to climb the stairs to her flat, but after a while became unable even to do that.

> My life was spent trying to complete the smallest tasks, going to the post office or getting a tiny amount of shopping in. Crawl downstairs. Stop. The kids on the estate used to laugh and shout abuse, because I was clearly quite poor. And I was always getting shoved about on the street. I had encounters with drunks and tramps. They tend to claim you as one of their own if you're tottering. My hips were so stiff that I rolled, and my legs stuck out at a peculiar angle. My absolute low point was seeing my reflection in a shop window: I looked like a crippled old lady.
>
> I was so lonely. Sometimes I wouldn't speak to anyone all day. I relied on people at bus stops for a chat, and I met some really wonderful people that way. People who touched my arm for a fleeing moment, which was

sometimes all I needed. Creatively I had shut down.

I finally went to the doctor and this was when I was told I had advanced osteoarthritis and needed both hips replaced. At the same time, a friend put me in touch with the Royal Ballet Benevolent Fund. That was the turning point. It gave me the financial help and emotional support I needed.

Ann continues her story telling how it took six months after the surgery, still walking with a stick but not in any pain, to try and get fit again. She joined a small professional class then bumped into an old friend who had returned to dancing at the age of fifty, and was keen for her to choreograph a solo piece for him.

The whole thing came to me one evening as I sat on the tube. It was based on upper-body work, using incredible leans and arcs. I left a message to say, 'James, call me.' But the next morning a colleague phoned to say that James was dead. Performing in Cologne that night, he'd misjudged a rail, fallen thirty feet and died instantly.

A year later, there was a memorial performance for him, and I performed the piece I wrote for him myself. I will never forget rediscovering the joy of dancing.

In losing and then finding my mobility again, I made the discovery that my body wasn't ME; it was simply something I put on. I feel very fortunate – I've been to this terribly dark place, where I felt I was nothing because I couldn't dance. But at the bottom of that dark place I found myself. And that has been an incredibly empowering experience.

Ann, now fifty-eight, has her own dance troupe, 'From Here to Maturity', and is currently on a national tour.

• • •

When I say *I* left my body, this is because it felt like it. It was me and not something abstract.

Sarah, on the way home from a walk in the countryside passed the house where one of the rooms was used as a church (RC). She called in to say a prayer although, as she says, she wasn't feeling religious; in fact, she says she felt 'particularly emotionally dry'. As she was praying, it felt as if she was talking to a wall, as if nobody was there or listening to her. 'I felt a bit frustrated and tried to force myself to feel a bit of emotion.'

> Instead of feeling anything, I left my body, like popping through a hole in a wall, suspended just below the ceiling. I was aware that I had left my body and, although I felt wonderful and right, without thinking I panicked to get back to my body. It was like swimming against the current to get back, but the whole thing probably didn't last longer than a second or two.

Rather shaken by the experience, Sarah then hurried home but didn't tell anyone about it except her husband, and that was a while later. She recalls not *seeing* anything and not feeling a 'tremendous emotion', but repeats, 'When I say *I* left my body and not "my soul left my body", this is because it felt like this; one thinks of one's soul as something detached, like a heart, but it was me and not something abstract.'[11]

As surely as there are experiences/stories that defy explanation, other than to be accepted as from the 'unnamed something', the 'universal energy', the 'life force', 'God' – years ago a group of nuns, without either money or building experience, decided to build their own chapel, their only asset belief in what they were doing, and in a 'higher guiding power'. Soon, and apparently 'out of the blue', materials and expertise arrived, and always just at the time they were needed; the nuns able to realise their ambition. At the present time, an American couple, devoting their lives to the care of street children in South America, having opened a home for these children have now also opened the first school. All donations are private, they have no government aid at all, yet, as they explained, 'Whenever a bill comes in, the right amount of money to cover that bill turns up' – so too perhaps, should we accept, as a touch of God's magic, all the strange yet wonderful phenomena we may be fortunate enough to experience from time to time.

Helen Johnson tells of an experience she had some years ago in Africa, where she then lived.

My husband and I were relaxing over our customary evening drink, and *The Sunday Times* crossword, when suddenly I was made conscious of a wonderful feeling of upliftment. A glow seemed to come over me (no, not the whisky!) and I asked my husband not to speak for a moment. A sense of power surged through me and, somewhat bewildered I tried to channel my thoughts into universal love. Certainly, I had perception of power beyond and greater than self. Slowly, the sensation faded away and my thoughts came back to normal. Disappointingly, I was tongue-tied when I endeavoured to explain what had happened to my husband, as he did not think along those lines at all. It was too precious an experience to tell to just anybody, so I kept it to myself for a very long time.

Being a Sunday night, with no staff, I went into the kitchen (partly because I wanted to be by myself) and cooked a positively inspired supper!

Now, when I become low-spirited, I try to look back on my experience and to realise that there must be something above our mundane life.[12]

Another lady tells us of her experience when she was looking after a Friends Meeting House, high on a spur of the forest.

Sleeping on a camp bed in the sitting room of the dwelling next door, one night I awoke slowly at about one o'clock to a feeling of absolute safety and happiness; everything in the world around me seemed to be singing, 'All is very well.' After an almost unbelievable few minutes I got up and went to the window and saw the valley filled with the love of God, flowing and spreading from the roadside and the few houses of the village. It was as though a great source of light and love and goodness was there along the valley, absolutely true and unchangeable. I went outside and looked down over the hedge, and the light and assurance were most truly there; I looked and looked, and, to be honest, I was not thankful, as I should have been, but trying to absorb the awareness of safety and joy so deeply that I would never forget it.

Next day I visited a paralysed, indeed dying, doctor, and as I waited in his kitchen for him to be ready to see me, I picked up an old *Reader's Digest* that his housekeeper was reading, open at an article on just such religious experiences as I had had the previous night. This convinced me I was quite sane and I even told the doctor something of my experience.[13]

The following very personal account is from a lady who believes she was put in touch with the 'ultimate reality', at a sad time in her life.

We came back from holiday to find that my mother had died unexpectedly and no one had been able to get in touch with us. I was then forty-four, very happily married, with three children, and a believing but somewhat detached Anglican. I can never remember a time when I doubted the existence of God, though I have not been able yet to feel the great compelling power which the person of Jesus exerts on so many. Belief in Christ as the Spirit of God is the nearest I can come to it.

It is difficult to write what came next. Anything one does write is totally inadequate and I was too shaken and disturbed to do so at the time. My remembrance now is inevitably coloured by subsequent reading of mystical literature, but at that time I had not the slightest idea that such literature existed and had never come across it. All I can truthfully say now, after several years, is that at some point in the next few days – even before the funeral, I think – I had the most shattering experience of my entire life. I believe it was during a sleepless night, but it seems to have been an experience entirely out of time as we accept the notion. Without any sense perception (except that I do seem to recollect an impression of light and darkness), I was made aware of a Reality beyond anything that my own mind could have conceived. And that Reality was a total love of all things in heaven and earth. 'It' enclosed and accepted every thing and every creature: there was no distinction of its love between the star, the saint and the torturer. All were 'kept' by this Power, and loved by it. I understood – then at least – the phrases 'I am that I am' and what I later read as 'the coincidence of opposites'. 'It' is Eternal Being.

There was much more, but somewhere in this time of dark night a symbol (a morning glory flower, as it happens) arose – from my subconscious, I suppose – which brought me a tremendous relief and comfort. I subsequently read of such happenings in Jung but, again, knew nothing of them at the time.

It was all overwhelming and psychologically terrifying; I was very frightened at the time that I was going mad. I quite accept that all this might well seem a natural reaction to shock and grief and guilt, and a self-induced comfort in a time of emotional and physical turmoil.

For myself, I did not doubt then, and have never doubted since, that I was put in touch with that ultimate reality for which we use the shorthand 'God'.[14]

• • •

The sudden smelling of an exquisite, soothing and uplifting perfume appears to be the more usual way for that 'little bit of magic' to reach us.

As I sat at my husband's bedside, holding his hand (he

was in intensive care having just undergone major surgery), full of fear and feeling almost paralysed with sadness and despair, a sudden explosion of the most beautiful perfume enveloped the two of us. Although present for only a moment, it brought for me a feeling of 'sweet calm' and the certainty that, whatever, we were not alone.

I asked the nurse standing nearby about the perfume, but all she did was shrug and say, 'There's no perfume in here!'

Two close friends seriously interested in all religions, and all things 'paranormal', were having coffee and an animated discussion on these subjects in a tiny jiffy burger in north London. Suddenly, above all the stench of frying fat and cigarette smoke, came the unmistakable smell of incense. Stopped in their track, speechless, the two of them stared at each other, then cautiously peered around the room; no one else had registered the smell, while the frying and smeech and cigarette smoke were in full swing as usual. The friends never forgot this experience and often marvelled at the power that must have been generated for them to register the smell of 'incense' in such a small enclosed space, with boiling fat and cigarette smells the norm.

After the sudden death of her four-and-a-half-year-old son, Joan Pemberton could find no comfort in anything or anyone. She tells us:

The Church seemed powerless to help me, as did the medical profession. I could not go out of the flat I was living in at that time and, although I tried very hard, I could see nothing but blackness and an intense longing to die. One morning I was dusting, tidying, the usual household chores, when I smelled the most wonderful garden flowers. It is difficult to describe the smell I mean – rather like a garden after rain. Being of a somewhat practical mind in such things, I looked around for the source of the smell. There were no flowers in the flat, certainly none outside, no perfumed polishes or toilet things in use. Then I sat down and for the first time since my son died I felt peaceful inside. I believe this was God's comfort; my son felt very near and I no longer felt alone.

All I can tell you now is that I have no fear of what we call death. To me it will be shedding the material life for a spiritual life and although I have had no great revelations, I shall try to live according to His divine plan and be ready to leave when He is ready for me.[15]

God's magic; all embracing, running through every beat of life, every circumstance.

Healing the physical

Not at all a religious person, Hilda Nuttal, suffering from chest problems, had such a vivid dream she had to tell people about it.

In her dream, Hilda knew that she was in bed, and that nuns were gathered around her, ministering to her. She watched them, and knew they were giving her some sort of healing. On waking, she felt well and refreshed, and believed it was because of the nuns.

Healing the emotions

Cheryl, a Canadian, remembers when she was thirteen years old, going through a very bad time in her life. She was placed in a care home and stresses how awful it was and how scared she was.

One night she woke up feeling really cold, unusual for her

she explained, and she saw her grandparents. Her grandfather was sitting on the edge of her bed while her grandmother stood behind him, just as in an old-fashioned photograph. It was the hardest time of her life, but they were trying to assure her with, 'It's OK.'

As young as she was, she remembers knowing that they were impressing her with the thought that everything would be all right.

God's magic, giving guidance

> After I felt the call of God to trust Him for everything, I was in the RAF as an aircraft mechanic. After a short time I was posted to the Far East and during the trouble we were required to keep up a fighter umbrella. This meant I had to decide which aircraft to service first and which had to be left to the last. Imagine a line of fighters as one taxies to the far end and one to the other. We were short staffed in my trade. I trusted God to guide me to the right plane and in my mind came a quiet voice. I obeyed the code letters and raced to that aircraft. As I did, my heart was filled with joy to the brim. After the trouble was over I worked it out to 360 aircraft checked without the mistake of servicing the wrong one. I can write a small book on how God had guided me and also fill it with everyday happenings which I know come from our Maker, not the subconscious.[16]

Similarly, Arthur Smith tells of his remarkable experience of 'guidance' while serving as a staff officer in France in the First World War. Badly wounded in the foot, the surgeon gave him the choice of 'leaving his foot on', but he might develop blood poisoning, or amputating it, but that would be the end of his service. Having until the next day to decide, he opened his Bible at random and at the page containing the phrase, ' The Lord is thy consolation and shall keep thy foot from being taken.' He refused the operation and lived to write his memoirs.

God's magic visible when in danger

When I was twenty-seven years, I was going through divorce and suffering great personal unhappiness, living in New York in a shabby and depressing hotel. One evening, after a lot to drink, I was sitting in bed having one last cigarette. That was the last thing I remembered. Next morning, when I awoke, the lamp beside me was still lit, there were cigarette ashes in the ashtray but no cigarette stub and no filter. There was a black hole in the straw mattress about an inch in diameter and an inch deep but no filter tip. The most amazing thing was that my nylon night dress was completely disintegrated on my right side yet I didn't have a burn or any other kind of mark on me. I had fallen asleep with a lighted cigarette in my hand on a straw mattress in a nylon night-dress.

At one point in the night I had a feeling that a man in a grey suit, surrounded by an aura of light, was standing in the room. He just stood there quietly, looking at me, and not saying anything. The vision lasted only a few seconds.[17]

God's magic for those given the privilege to 'see'

An American, Bridget Riley, now living in Florida, gives us this story that happened when she was a teenager and carrying more books to school than she could cope with. As she struggled onto the bus, and just before taking a seat at the front, she took a quick look at two people dressed in white who were sitting on the back seat. They were the image of her two grandparents who had passed on. Then she heard the woman speak, 'I think she saw us.' She thought this was strange, it didn't make sense; of course as a fellow passenger on the bus she had seen them. Later, she had the thought to go back and speak to them, but then the bus driver's voice came loud and clear, 'Fifty-sixth street, your street, little girl.'

She had a great struggle getting off the bus with all her books and then she looked up to see the old lady handing her purse to her through the open window. She had forgotten to pick it up. The bus was gone, and so were the elderly couple, before she could say a proper thank you.

Next day, she asked some regulars on the bus if they knew the elderly couple. She even asked the driver, explaining that the person she was asking about was the old lady who had handed her purse to her through the open window, the day before. No one knew them.

Again she spoke to the driver, 'Surely you remember the lady handing me my purse through the open window, yesterday?' 'No I don't,' he growled, 'and my bus is air-conditioned – the windows don't go down.'

Jackie Humphries, who lives in Devon, couldn't pull herself together. Devastated after a horrendous car crash killed her eighteen-year-old son and three of his friends in 1991, the following year, at Christmas time, she took a holiday with her husband to the Canary Islands, hoping the change would help her in some way.

On the 27th December, at 11.00 a.m. she was lying on a sun bed, in the sun. Her husband had put on some music and she was trying to relax. She felt a shadow right over her at the end of the sun bed. She opened her eyes to see a massive angel standing at the bottom of the bed. He was about seven feet tall and she stresses knowing it was a 'he'. He had a beautiful face with long, curly blonde hair, and it was all so startling and amazing she couldn't speak.

Closing her eyes, she kept repeating in her head, 'Go away, go away,' but when she dared to open her eyes again, he was still there. It all lasted about a minute, but she remembers the feeling with it was all 'love'. 'The most beautiful, wonderful feeling, and love, not of this world.' She remembers sobbing, 'All love, love, love.' Jackie couldn't tell her husband about this experience for a few days.

A well known author's friend Mary, another writer, and Mary's sister, helped many Jewish people to escape Nazi Germany just before the outbreak of the war. Years later, Mary featured in *This is Your Life*, and her author friend, plus many other friends who watched the programme, saw a man standing behind Mary's chair who had helped her from the Berlin side, been captured, and shot by the SS.

God's Magic, visible in the tiny, unexpected, and ordinary incidents of life; a sudden whiff of pipe smoke in the kitchen telling her that her father was near.

The significance in seeing a heart shape built out of 'anything'; steam on a mirror, a leaf, a pattern on a carpet, but unmistakable, and bringing comfort, usually at a time of worry or uncertainty.

The lady who received so much evidence and so many answers from the other side of life that she almost believed she was on a 'hot-line'.

The artist who paints the future. He has revelations of future events during the sleep state and paints them immediately on waking.

The ordinary incidents of life; the super ordinary; gelling together in a diversity of experience that *is* life. John Lennon tellingly remarked, 'Life is what happens when you are busy making other plans.' Many people accept life as 'just life', and travel along not looking for any meaning other than to live out their allotted life span to the best of their ability, and that's it. Finished. The end. No more. The purpose, the loves, the strivings, the successes, the failures, in the final analysis amount to nothing. Everything in a time slot which is, itself, nothing.

Then there are stories; tales, experiences, which, touching even the most cynical and closed of minds cause a little stirring, a little hesitation, as the afterthought is expressed: 'I don't believe in anything, but...!' Experiences as incredible as they are welcome, as fascinating as they are inspiring: 'I was at the bottom of a black pit'; 'it was the worst moment of my life'. Experiences; the moment of moments; the highest, the lowest point in a life, and incredibly, an opportunity for the magic to steal in. Possibly in the form of an ultra-real, soft, soothing embrace; or as a sudden jolt of awakening, understanding, certainty. A certainty of being 'upheld by a power', given strength; a certainty of there being a reason for everything; and the certainty that we do not face life alone.

Life: the oddest, weirdest, most wonderful, unexpected and mysterious of anything we will ever encounter. Life; shining through every moment, every emotion, the highs, the lows: the unimaginable way things have of working out, enticing us on, giving us hope. And in the amazing way that only life itself can conjure up, possibly in some strange circumstance, or in something as ordinary as meeting a friend for a cup of coffee; or perhaps through the emotion of the inner self, anyone of us can, at any time, touch the 'true' self, and find that we too are 'leaning on the invisible'.

Partakers of what can only be termed God's magic. The magic that is God.

Chapter Six

---

*'There's nothing left for me, of days that used to be, except
a memory among my souvenirs. A photograph or two...'*

SPIRIT PHOTOGRAPHY, OR SPIRIT extras appearing on
photographs, was very much in the news around 1862, only
twenty-three years after the invention of photography itself.

William H Mumler, an engraver by trade, and a knowledgeable
amateur photographer, produced the first so-called 'spirit
photograph' in Boston, USA. Mumler was followed by a series
of psychic photographers all of whom (including Mumler
himself), were later exposed as frauds.

At one point, however, when Mumler was prosecuted for fraud,
the highest court in the United States found him not guilty. Sadly,
he was later disgraced because of a photograph he took of a
Japanese family whose daughter appeared as an 'extra' on the
photograph, and she was still living. The fact that she was
thousands of miles away at the time the picture was taken was
ignored. (Astral travelling, or the ability of the spirit body to travel
away from the physical body was not as well known then as it
is today.)

The excitement caused by the seemingly overwhelming
evidence for the genuineness of psychic photography, and then
the disillusionment as one after another of the practitioners were
found to be fraudulent, caused a setback in the development of

the phenomena which did not recover for years; but a lingering interest remained, and the millions of deaths during WWI. gave rise to a strong revival of spirit photography in Europe. Now, in our modern world, with its state-of-the-art technology – including recording equipment, digital cameras and web-cams, interest in all things paranormal has returned with a vengeance.

In 1963, the Rev Kenneth Lord took a photograph of the beautiful altar of the church in Newby, Yorkshire. When the photograph was developed it showed a transparent figure in a monk's cowl, his face turned towards the camera. Submitting the photograph to the Home Office laboratory (which had enhancing equipment), the experts concluded that even the most rigorous computer analysis could not reproduce such an image, and that it was probably genuine.

One of the most famous photographs of spirit extras was taken in December 1924 from the rear deck of the American oil tanker Watertown.

Two seamen had been killed by poisonous fumes when cleaning a cargo tank. They were buried at sea. The next day the first mate reported seeing two faces following the ship; soon, everyone on board saw them as, day after day, the two faces reappeared, following in the ship's wake.

In New Orleans, the captain reported what was happening to the owners. They handed him a sealed roll of film and asked for the first mate to try and take a photograph of the phenomena with his camera.

When the ship left for the Panama Canal, the mate took six photographs of the heads as they continued to follow the ship, appearing just above the waves.

The film was handed over to a company representative on its return to New Orleans. Five of the photographs were blank but the sixth showed two faces that everyone agreed were the faces of the dead men.

The photograph has become a classic piece of evidence for psychical research.

No one in the family can remember when the spirit extra appeared on the photograph of the elderly couple featured in the picture section. They are standing in front of the coal-house door which was situated directly opposite their house, one in a seemingly never-ending street of houses, typical of mining villages in the north east of England. Their granddaughter thinks she recognises the spirit extra as being that of her great-grandmother, whose image she recalls from a huge framed photograph that hung on the walls of her grandmother's house for years.

To pick out faces or meaningful images from say, a carpet, or a plastered wall, or a photograph, is apparently not to see 'spirit'. But could there be a reason for unusual phenomena appearing? Heidi believes so.

After her dad died, the family, still grieving, decided to spend the second anniversary of his death in a happy way, celebrating his life instead of, in Heidi's words, 'moping around'.

Having enjoyed a meal in a favourite pub, Heidi, her two sisters and their mother strolled into the garden to give a toast. Raising their glasses to the sky, they called out, 'Cheers, Dad, we love you,' then Heidi captured each one of them in a photograph on her digital camera. But when she looked at her mum's photograph on the screen of her camera, she was shocked.

Calling to the others, they crowded round to look, silent for a moment as they tried to take in what they were seeing. There, clearly showing around the head of their mother were seemingly 'angel's wings'. Heidi quickly took another snap of her mother but that came out as normal.

Word soon spread around the pub and people came out to have a look at this extraordinary photograph. Someone made the suggestion that it could be cigarette smoke. They took another picture of her mum with someone standing close by smoking, but it wasn't the same.

Her mum was due to go into hospital in three days for an examination and she was frightened about it, but Heidi reported that, after seeing the photograph she felt calm, knowing her husband was there looking after her.

In 1995, as fire swept through the old town hall of Wem, Shropshire, Tony O'Rahilly stood watching by the roadside before returning to his car, parked nearby, to collect his camera. An amateur photographer, Tony always carried a camera with him and today's picture of the blaze that he captured proved to be perhaps the scoop of a lifetime.

When processed, the film showed the eerie face of a young girl, dressed in old-fashioned costume, standing in the doorway of the town hall's fire escape. Tony was both shocked and amazed to see the figure, which appears both on the photograph and on the negative. He sent the photograph off to the Association for the Scientific Study of Anomalous Phenomena, and the Royal Photographic Society.

Both groups returned the same verdict. It was a genuine photo, with no tampering or special effects.

Yet there was still some disagreement. Could this have been a natural trick of the light, the twist of the flames and the shadows of the building forming an outline of a little girl? Painstaking research found the negative to be genuine.

A tiny plaque stating that the town hall had been burned down in 1677 was one of the few things that survived the fire. Gradually, the history of the first fire revealed that it had been started by a fourteen-year-old girl called Jane Churm, who accidentally set fire to the thatched roof of her home with a candle. The resulting blaze virtually wiped out the town, but claimed only one life. A historian has confirmed that the 'ghost' is wearing a dress from that era.

Viv Halliday treasures the photograph of her uncle, Nelson Emmerson, the soldier seen proudly wearing the uniform of the Coldstream Guards, and the snap shot of her aunt, Nelson's sister-in-law, taken on a coach trip in the early 'sixties. Sadly Nelson was killed in action at Caen, France, on 10th August 1944. His 'spirit' photograph appears on the snapshot and was immediately recognised by his widow, Viv's aunt, Mary Emmerson. Other photographs on the same roll of film were apparently normal.

Unfortunately, but part of the fascination with this spirit extra, is the fact that 'now you see it, now you don't'; but when you do (see it), you see an amazing tiny – barely a half inch – replica of Nelson, the soldier, down to his waist. Clearly visible is the head and the badge on the collar; on the tunic, the Coldstream Guards buttons are seen lined as they are in twos; part of the wide white belt is visible and the pattern on the sleeve as he holds his arm in front.

Nelson is seen clearly marked by a blue circle on the second snapshot for those who have not been able to visualise it at first.

Many people are now noticing orbs or 'round lights' appearing on photographs, especially, it seems, photographs that have been taken at a castle or some other historic sight. While there is probably a rational and natural explanation for most of these phenomena, dust on the lens, processing flaws, etc. there are many cases of orbs or lights being unidentified, unexplainable (perhaps photographic proof of the presence of spirit energies), and therefore left to the interpretation of the viewer.

In March 2003, strange, disturbing goings-on were reported by workers at the start of deep excavation work underneath Edinburgh Castle. Workers reported a disquiet; sudden severe coldness, chilling and at times almost incapacitating; a strong feeling of a 'presence' so unnerving and overpowering that men were refusing to work in certain areas of the excavation. Lights appeared from nowhere, moving, hovering – sometimes appearing as an ethereal 'shimmering' glow.

The photograph you see in the picture section of an orb is one of many taken by officials involved in the excavation work at the castle, and by Scottish Television, who broadcast the happenings on one of their news programmes.

Many years ago, far back into the last century, it was forecast that whereas this new century of 2000 would see man continuing the great progress already made in technology, it would also see a return to spirituality. It was even forecast that there would be a spiritual revolution.

Having thought about, and perhaps come to the conclusion that this is now happening as we witness a restlessness, a searching, a seeking for something more than our material world has to offer, we are perhaps also seeing a gradual softening and 'guarded acceptance' by science of the possibilities of the unexplainable; the existence of other spheres. (Recently we have seen the first artificial limb, an arm, motivated by the power of thought.)

We are now witnessing what may be an unparalleled materialising of paranormal activity; possibly there to give us pause for thought, encouragement in our seeking, or simply to give assurance that in our clever, technological, scientific age, the wisdom of the spiritual will not be ignored or put to one side.

Evidence of a spiritual realm is manifesting through countless channels including healing, apparitions, and recordings, both sound and visual. All manner of phenomena there for our consideration.

'Except you see signs and wonders, you will not believe'
words taken from the Bible; John, ch.4 v.48.

Since the first scientific information was produced in 1898, scientists still cannot agree on the validity of the Turin Shroud, despite years of rigorous tests being carried out (although in the results of the most recent tests produced in 1978 there does seem to have been more evidence for its authenticity than against).

The Turin Shroud is claimed to be the white burial cloth Jesus was wrapped in when he was laid in the tomb; so-called due to its present home in Turin, where it has lain since 1578. Science has proved that the cloth contains the image of a man who was executed under the Roman capital punishment of crucifixion. There are blood stains on the cloth from scourging; crucifixion wounds in the wrists and feet, and wounds from small sharp objects all over the head.

In 1978, probably the most important conclusion drawn from five days of intensive experiments is that the body image of the cloth is definitely not a painting and not made by the application of any foreign material. Nobody knows for sure how the image was made, and nobody has been able to reproduce an image remotely like that of the Shroud. A misunderstanding between researchers regarding the dating (of the Shroud) has now been partly clarified and all evidence, including manuscripts and miniature drawings from the twelfth century (and earlier?), point to the fact that the image on the Turin Shroud is the image taken from the body of Christ.

Incomprehensible astounding evidence, from the holiest of relics, to a humble spirit extra appearing on a photograph. Images of controversy, but, to many, undeniable proof of so-called 'supernatural intervention'.

And so, with all the amazing technology we now have at our disposal, what might we expect to witness, albeit in the distant future? Closer links being forged with the other side (of life)? Serious forages into time travel? Travelling by the power of thought? Not forgetting it is we ourselves – each one of us – who are believed to be the most miraculous of all creation. With our consciousness ever expanding and wide open, in other words, with an open mind; an open, enquiring mind, and a sincere and loving heart, is anything impossible? Is everything possible? Who knows!

A photograph; a souvenir of days gone by recreating memories, shading lives, giving substance to who we are.

A photograph; one with a tiny, almost indiscernible spirit extra bridging the two worlds; comforting, soothing, uplifting. Giving hope to a broken heart...

Simply a photograph.

Chapter Seven

Going Home

On the 1st day of February 2003, seven crew members perished in the Columbia space craft disaster. President Bush, in his speech following the disaster, comforted the nation with the words:

'The crew did not return safely to earth, but we can pray that they are safely home.'

SINCE THE BEGINNING, MAN has accepted, however seriously, the concept of 'going home' at the time of death. Art and literature have expounded the belief over the centuries, and acceptance of the 'other side of life' as a truth, a reality, is the basis of most religions.

Those who do not believe in the continuation of life in the spiritual sense, who cannot recognise man as a spiritual being in a physical body, might possibly see a regeneration of life as in nature; in the miraculous re-birth that follows a long hard winter; in the fact that all substance is changed but not lost. Energy is never lost, it is transformed. Others might see 'living on' as in heredity; the continuation of life in the family line. Another thought is survival through legacy; a writer in his books, an artist in his pictures, and perhaps, for the majority of us, our influence in one way or another; in the way we have touched other lives.

There are people who believe in the theory of reincarnation – a theory that some of us, if not all, return to earth perhaps many times to re-learn lessons failed in the past, likening this earth plane of ours to a school-room.

And many believe there are those who, having now passed through the portals of so-called death, return – thus proving survival. Evidence of survival comes in so many different ways they are impossible to quantify or classify, and despite years of research on the subject, scientists are still divided as to the findings.

Montague Keen made his living as a farmer and agricultural writer. An intelligent and dedicated man, he had held a senior post with the National Farmers' Union, but the study of paranormal phenomena was his true life's work. He investigated reports of paranormal happenings from all over the world and served on the council of the Society for Psychical Research for fifty-five years, putting all the cases he investigated to the utmost scrutiny.

Moments before his death in January 2004, Montague had been involved in a passionate debate on the paranormal at the Royal Society of Arts headquarters in London. As his body lay on the floor – he had suffered a sudden heart attack – and just before he passed away, he turned to his wife Veronica, and in a private gesture, reaffirmed a pact he had made with her some years earlier. Both had promised that whoever died first would attempt to send a message from beyond the grave.

Scientists in America now claim to have substantial evidence of the return of Montague Keen and of his determination to fulfil his promise. Led by Professor Gary Schwartz of the University of Arizona, and using some of the most rigorous scientific tests ever devised to research the paranormal, Professor Schwartz claims, 'Montague still exists. It's clear to me he is continuing his work from the other side. He is passing information to us through spiritual mediums.' The professor goes on to explain that, as a scientist, he has to be neutral and unbiased in his work, but that the data given by Monty has convinced him of survival after death.

Messages began returning to his wife Veronica from mediums all over the world. At first they were hesitant and garbled, but soon they became clearer and focused. 'Monty described his death to several mediums.' Veronica, who still lives in North London, reported. 'He told one that he was bitterly upset when I was moved away from him as he was dying.' And another that he wanted her to convert his ashes into a diamond, which was to be worn as a necklace. Veronica was stunned by the message; 'Monty and I were discussing this in bed the night before he died,' she explained. Soon Professor Schwartz, who had met Montague during the course of his research, heard of the evidence being relayed to Veronica and immediately saw the value of trying to make contact with him in the afterlife. 'Montague was a renowned psychic investigator, if anyone could communicate after they died, it would be him.' It was at this point that the Professor began his scientifically controlled study of Montague's apparent return.

Part of the evidence gained was Montague accurately describing his death and where it had happened. He also described the manner of his father's death in World War II. Also correctly stated was the fact that Veronica had installed new blinds in her house a few days previously, and he correctly predicted that an article about his death would appear in the *Daily Mail* newspaper. From being more than eighty per cent correct, the information transmitted by Montague, during a re-run of the experiments, was more than ninety per cent accurate, some of it being even more specific.

Encouraged by the evidence, Professor Schwartz began to question Monty about life beyond the grave, finding that: 'Monty was surprised about how similar to 'real' life the afterlife appeared to be. He was surprised about how easy it was to 'experience' being with Veronica and life in general. It's almost as if he's walking among us. He says that time does not exist in the afterlife in the same way it does for us. He experiences time because it affects those he loves, not because it affects him directly.'

Professor Schwartz, who has a doctorate from Harvard University, has served as professor of Psychiatry at Yale University and as director of one of America's foremost behavioural medicine clinics; has edited eleven academic books and published more than 400 scientific papers, has not been an easy man to convince of the afterlife. He is now planning to extend his work in this area with Montague's help, and that of other spirits and to build up a comprehensive picture of what he believes to be the afterlife. And through presenting such evidence to the world, he hopes to persuade even the most cynical minds that we are only just beginning to understand the nature of the human soul.

For Veronica, Montague's widow, the results of the professor's work have had a deep impact. She is now convinced that her husband is still with her in spirit form, testimony to their enduring love.

'People assume that only the young can love this deeply,' she says. 'It's not true. We are soul mates that should never be apart. We are still connected emotionally and spiritually. I miss him so much. My one consolation is he says he can't wait to show me around the spirit world. We travelled all around the globe together, so eternity has to be next.'[1]

• • •

Evidence gathered from first-hand accounts of death bed scenes are too numerous and detailed to be ignored. Here we find authenticity for much of what we have been taught to believe since childhood – that we go to another world when we die. Yet life, with all its trials and tribulations, so often tempers the spirit (the real you and I?), obscuring that sublime innocence of belief we once had in accepting heaven as our home. Mother Teresa, our modern-day saint, wanted, more than anything, to touch people's souls to prepare them for the next world; as in every age there have been men and women whose shining faith and example have uplifted and encouraged others to believe in the 'unnamed something', the 'universal energy', the 'life-force', 'God'.

Customs, rites, ceremonies, may vary at the time of a passing; in the Tibetan Book of the Dead we are told of a ceremony where the top of the head is examined to determine if the spirit has departed from the deceased. Until recent times, nurses in hospitals were advised to be sure a window was left open for the spirit to depart. (A lady from Sheffield tells of how, on a bitterly cold New Year's Eve, the outside door of the house blew open, just as her mother passed.)

Although customs may vary, there is a broad outline, a similarity running through all practices at the moment of death, as there is in the understanding of our next place of abode and the description of the journey there; all depending on our culture, and added to that, on our own personal illumination. From the Gitanjali we read:

Bid me farewell, my brothers. I bow to you all and take my departure. A summons has come and I am ready for my journey.

At this time of my parting, wish me good luck, my friends. The sky is flushed with the dawn and my path lies beautiful. Ask not what I have to take there. I start my journey with empty hands and expectant heart.

I was not aware of the moment when I first crossed the threshold of this life. In death the same unknown will appear as ever known to me. And because I loved this life, I know I shall love death as well.

Possibly because they had such a cruel life here on the earth plane, the old Negro spiritual slave songs were full of the words 'going home', and of rowing across the Jordan to freedom, and the 'real' life on the other side. Some years ago, Stephen was ill and near to his time of passing. Sitting on the sofa at home, he suddenly sat forward and stared high into a corner of the room. Then he started the steady, rhythmic motion of rowing, arms moving together smoothly as he pulled on the oars; obviously trying to reach somewhere, he rowed, pulling away, eyes fixed firmly on a distant shore.

Farraday, the famous scientist who lived in Victorian times, belonged to a small religious sect who taught him not to make too much of death, seeing it as a mere passing.[2] In modern-day thinking, a significant amount of verse and poetry describe death as 'nothing at all', simply the 'going into another room'; moving into another state of reality; a place where the departed ones are 'citizens of heaven', and a place where, according to innumerable accounts, the two worlds (ours and the next), impinge on each other. For just as mankind transforms into spirit, so too does all life have a counterpart on the other side. (Recently, a gentle and caring lady whose dog was about to pass, in her heartache, lovingly held the animal and asked her if she really had to go, to try and come back to let her 'mum' know she was safe. She returned, two weeks later, at a friend's house.)

Evidence is not difficult to come by as to the 'superimposed' health condition of many about to depart, hours, or sometimes days before passing. Reports include having a strong desire, and often the energy, to put everything in order; looking better than they had done for months:

Do you know why I knew that the Bishop was dying? I found him so beautifully transformed that I had the idea that he couldn't live. He was beautiful, too beautiful.[3]

Suddenly he was his usual old loving self. Age fifty-seven, he had born his terrible two-year illness calmly, patiently, not troubling anyone. There was a strictness about his demeanour, that's all, that reminded me somehow of an old-fashioned headmaster. But then, days before his passing, the old Peter briefly returned and I knew it was the end.

At the last moment, when his breathing told us this was it, he opened his eyes and looked straight at my mother. Eyes that hadn't opened for days did, and they weren't chalky or vague. They were clear and blue and full of love, and then they closed with his last breath. If a death can be lovely, his was.

The greatest gift you could have given me, my mother managed to say to him through tears, through 'I love you', through the towering beauty of that last moment. The hush in the room broken then by quiet crying.

My father told me when I was small that I didn't need to stand on my toes to touch God, because He is everywhere. He was right. He was in that room.

In his last moment my father taught me that there is nothing stronger than love between two people. It reaches past death and cradles hearts that weep. The last thing he did in this world was to show my mother how entwined their souls are…and it was everything.[4]

· · ·

There is an old saying: 'Coming events cast their shadows before.' Millie Sutcliffe had a son who was studying art in Germany. She knew her son was ill, but on seeing a photograph sent over to her from Germany, something told her that her son was dying. A short time later, she reports that, on 10th April, 'At half past four, I was in my bedroom at home in Liverpool. I felt as if a great, strong, cold wind came through that house, lifted me up and laid me across the bed. For fifteen or twenty minutes, not a muscle in my body was capable of movement. That was the time, I discovered later, when Stuart was dying.'[5]

'Coming events cast their shadows' is a truth often shown in signs, warnings, premonitions; when sensitive people, or people in a sensitive state, can say seemingly meaningless things, but things that portend that which is about to come.

A young woman dying with cancer startled her husband by asking for her hair rollers, then struggled to put them in, saying she had to look her best as she was going somewhere special. She passed a short time later. A man one morning, told his wife that something special was going to happen that day, attended the football match as usual and died there during the game. Harry Chandler, a man in his fifties, exclaimed to someone that he was not afraid to meet his maker only days before his sudden passing. Two neighbours stood respectfully watching the funeral of another neighbour, admiring the flowers, the younger one remarking that she would love to have such beautiful flowers at her own funeral, passed suddenly a few days later, and got her wish.

The evidence of loved ones who have passed appearing to those about to make their transition is full and plenty. Two brothers died of scarlet fever within twenty-four hours of each other in places twenty-four miles apart. Four-year-old David, who was the second to die, stood up in his bed about an hour before his passing and pointed to the foot of the bed. He told his parents that he saw his little brother Harry, who had come to fetch him, standing there. Their parents had deliberately kept Harry's death secret from David in order not to hinder his chances of recovery.

In the presence of witnesses, a woman in the last seconds of life looked up and said, 'There's John,' and then passed away. John was her brother who had died just the week before – but she had not been told about his death. Warnings, premonitions, signs that give comfort to those left behind who, because of such incidents, feel that, after all, there must be 'something there'.

A nurse, aged twenty-three was assisting at a heart operation on a baby four weeks old, but the baby died. The surgeon showed the abnormality of the heart to her and two other nurses, then, in her own words:

Suddenly the room and theatre were permeated with the scent of violets and the almost tangible sense of peace. The surgeon, a hard-bitten Australian, commented on the scent. No source could be found.

Since this time I have felt no pain at any death. I am sure of the presence of – who knows? Love, peace, God?

I have no personal fear of death despite threats of hell and purgatory in my life prior to this event. No longer do I fear, or feel angry with God because of a child's death... . The peace is still with me. I have never discussed this experience with anyone other than the staff present at the time. All had smelled the perfume. This has always puzzled, not obsessed me, but has upheld my faith in love.[6]

Perhaps the most usual evidence gained at a passing is when, just at that moment, that last moment, the patient looks up into a corner of the room and calls out, 'Mother,' or the name of some other loved one who, it seems, has come to 'take them' to the other side. A son reported that his mother, in the moments immediately before she died, looked upward and said, 'Oh, it's so beautiful!'

The following detailed account of a passing is from a nurse working at the Westminster hospital where she was caring for a patient who was dying of cancer:

> She (the patient), looked old and pale and never smiled or spoke to anyone. She became unconscious and was given the last rites. The daughter came to visit and the curtains were round to screen her from the other patients. We looked at her for a few moments; she looked the same – lined, drawn face, eyes closed. I said to the daughter, 'Come and have a cup of tea'...I drew the curtains round the bed again and we walked towards the door of the ward. I stopped suddenly.

> Something made me stop and I said, 'No, come back quickly' –and hurried to the bedside again. When we got there (the patient's) eyes were open and she looked quite conscious. She was smiling a wonderful smile and as I watched, her face became pink, the lines disappeared. She wriggled and stretched like a child waking up after a deep sleep, and suddenly she looked years younger and beautiful. Then staring up at a spot above the curtain rail at the end of her bed she stretched out her arms as if greeting someone she loved. She could see someone – I looked to see if I could too – I couldn't and yet I knew someone was there. I can remember

feeling a marvellous warm happiness inside me and all around. Then (the patient) lay back and was dead.[7]

James was a man with no faith, but he marvelled at the experience he had at the passing of his sister. Dying with TB, she struggled to say something to him and he held her up by the shoulders, she had no strength at all. Then, amazingly, she gave a convulsive start and stretched her arms out in welcome to the open window. Aware of a power that gave her strength to lift her arms, he says he will never forget her indescribable look of utter joy and shining eyes; the peace, the happiness, as she responded to a vision of 'welcome'. Then she closed her eyes, and passed away.[8]

Maggie Smith, a young nurse of nineteen was privileged enough to 'see' the spirit form of a patient leave the body. Here is her account of what happened.

> I was a night nurse in a hospital and was asked to sit with a patient who was dying. The ward was very quiet with only a shaded night-light, enough to administer to the patient. The patient died at 2.30 a.m. much to my annoyance as I was officially off duty at 3.00 a.m. To save myself some work I decided to report the death nearer three o'clock. Then I saw a strange thing happen. About 2.50 a.m. I saw another body hovering above the dead body. Complete in length, thickness and contour, except that it was translucent. This I saw very clearly. In my ignorance I thought it was the body cooling down but when it moved, undulating towards the foot of the bed I began to think about it.

She realised that she had seen the spirit depart from the body, and recorded that she was not dreaming, and she was not afraid.[9]

Kevin Johnston, knowing his father's time to pass was near, asked the other side of life, in his thoughts, if he could be present when it happened, so that he could help his father; but Kevin got more than he bargained for!

A young man who had travelled widely as a seaman, in the early 'nineties, Kevin found himself living and working twelve miles or so from his home town in the north of England. One of the younger members of a large Catholic family, he had never enjoyed an easy relationship with his father. In fact, over recent years, he had had little contact with him. He did know that he was ill, but how ill, he was uncertain. A developing medium, Kevin felt the urge, the need, to make peace with his father and try to help him, but he didn't know how to approach the situation. He sent his thoughts (prayers) out to spirit saying, 'If he needs me, I will help him.'

Within one week of doing this, he lost his job (not his fault), his flat had to go (it was with the job), and he had no choice but to move back home.

He found that his father was dying, but Kevin was pleased to have the chance to nurse him and 'put things right' between them, as he realised that it was mainly his own fault that they had had such a poor relationship.

They had one week together before he died. They talked and talked and made peace with each other, Kevin praying that he could be with his father when his time came.

At three a.m. one morning something woke him and he heard the words, 'Get up, it's time.' And so it was. He was with his father, comforting him and loving him, for fifteen minutes until, as Kevin expressed it, 'it was time for him to "go home" '.

Not to be left out, there are many stories of animals playing a part at a passing, and Smokey the cat was no exception.

My father was very ill with pancreatic cancer and we

knew we were about to lose him. We were sitting with him in the lounge when his cat Smokey walked towards us. Instead of heading in a straight line he seemed to veer off, as though skirting round something we couldn't see. Minutes later my brother David and I heard voices speaking quietly. We couldn't tell what they were saying. Then my dad took his last breath. Some people will be cynical, but David and I believe that we, and Smokey, sensed the spirits who'd come to help Dad on his way.

An American lady gives a most dramatic account of her husband's death bed scene as she tried to comfort him, and even go a little way with him, on his journey to the other side.

It was in New York City, and as her husband lay dying in a hospital room, June took his hand and closed her eyes. She felt herself being swiftly propelled into a vast current into space – an out-of-this-world feeling. Love was its force – the speed of it as though 'I were travelling a million miles a second'. June explains that her husband had always feared death, and she felt as if she was accompanying him and was closer to him in love and spirit 'than ever in our actual lives. The energy of this vast stream of upwards and outer spacial experience frightened me as I was aware that if I held on to my husband's hand too long I would be unable to return. I felt that as my husband had always feared death, I had gone a short way with him to comfort him. Plainly to me, God knew my desire, and answered it.'[10]

Billy Graham, the famous evangelist, recalls the day his grandmother died. He sat by her side in a dark room when suddenly the room seemed to glow with some sort of light. He tells us how his grandmother sat up in bed, even though she had been too weak to do so earlier and said, 'I see Jesus. He has his hand outstretched toward me.'

Then she saw Ben, her dead husband, who had lost a leg and

an eye in the Civil War. 'There's Ben,' she said, 'and he has both of his eyes and both of his legs!' Then, as Billy Graham recounts, his grandmother died, and the room once again became dark.[11]

Time, it goes without saying, plays an important part in each of our lives, and no more so than in our modern world. But what exactly *is* time? The author Allegra Taylor, talking about the capricious nature of time, explains, 'If we can't make sense of it as it exists on this little planet of ours, how are we expected to come to grips with the timelessness of eternity?' We can't even begin to comprehend the notion of a 'light year', the distance travelled by a beam of light in one year. The American lady, in her out-of-body experience mentioned earlier, felt as if she had travelled a million miles a second. She had lost all sense of time during her experience, and we are told that time does not exist as we know it on the other side of life. Time is altogether a strange experience when we consider it. A week can seem like a month, and vice versa, all depending on the state of mind and circumstance; but time also brings us to the question of fate. Is there such a thing as a time, a plan, for our birth and for our death? We read in the Bible;

> To everything there is a season, and a time to every purpose under the heaven: A time to be born, and a time to die;[12]

(During the Second World War Thomas Atkins, a sailor, was torpedoed twice and survived. On his second night home on leave he was caught up in a bomb blast and killed.) Accepting the words from the Bible to be true, can we then consider the age-old question: 'Do we have any say at all in our lives?' (It is strange how, in a certain situation, we do our best to resolve things as we want them to be, or as we think best; or maybe it is something we are particularly striving for. We can push and pull, scheme, insist, do any manner of things, but no matter how hard we try, no matter how desperate are our efforts, if it is not meant to happen, then it won't. Or, if we *do* succeed – in whatever it is that is seemingly not meant to happen ! – and it wasn't perhaps the right thing at the right time, it will fall apart, undo itself, be nothing but trouble, and we will end up wishing we hadn't succeeded in the first place!!) It is ironic that often (and it could be at a much later date) we clearly see the reason why such and such a thing failed to happen, and have to agree that it would not have been the right thing for us, after all. Religion teaches us that we have free will, we make the choices. In the words of a priest, 'At the heart of what it means to be human is the power to choose.' The word fate means 'Power predetermining events from eternity'. Could fate explain precognition? Precognition comes from a variety of sources including astrology, fortune-telling, clairvoyance.

There is a strong belief that we all, symbolically, have a clock above our heads, and that this clock stands for where we must be at a certain time in our lives. A while ago, Diana left London in the month of December, having worked there for a number of years, to return home to the North of England and plan her wedding for May. A friend who was a clairvoyant told her the 'time' was not right for the wedding. Probably on seeing the look of worry on her face at his words, he quickly explained about the clock which is 'symbolically' above our heads, and assured her that he didn't mean the wedding wouldn't happen, just that it wasn't the right time.

Forgetting all about this conversation after she returned home, Diana arranged her wedding for 2nd May and amazingly, all went to plan – until three days before the event. The wedding was cancelled. It did take place however, two months later, on 2nd July of the same year.

Having a clock above our heads, therefore having to be at a

certain place at a certain time in our lives, could conceivably endorse the more (to many) believable view that, yes, the broad outline of our lives is ordained… 'A time to be born; our family; the partner (soul-mate) we travel with; a time to die;' but we fill in the rest, moving from one pathway to another, perhaps feeling a 'prod' here, a pull there, and hopefully finding a guiding hand (if we ask for it) in all our endeavours. A time for that which has to be, and a time for free will; the little incidents and large events, amassing into what we hope will be a triumphant life, that is both freely chosen, yet existing within a divine framework – created by a far wiser mind than ours.

Although it seems that time, as we know it, does not exist on the other side of life, evidence suggests that spirit people, 'citizens of heaven', are aware of time in that it affects those they love, not because it affects them directly. Evidence also suggests that they are made unhappy if friends and loved ones on the earth plane seemingly 'shut them out', ignore them; rarely mentioning them by name or including them in their lives; in other words, treating them as 'dead'. In his book *Many Mansions*, published in 1943, Lord Dowding writes that there is evidence of:

> widespread grief and despondency among spirits recently departed from this life because, although they can see and mingle with those left behind, they cannot communicate to them that all is well, nor assuage their grief.

A recent poem expresses the same sentiment with the words:

> Speak to me in the easy way which you always used: put no difference in your tone. Wear no forced air of sorrow:

laugh as we always laughed at the little jokes we enjoyed together.

Pray, smile, think of me, pray for me. Let my name be ever the household word that it always was.[13]

A charity Child Bereavement Trust (CBT), set up to train doctors, nurses and professionals to help families through the pain of a child's death, realises the importance of grieving but remembering. *A Heartbeat Away*, recently published by the charity, is an anthology compiled by Sue Lane Fox, whose twenty-five-year-old son Harry was killed six years ago in a car crash. She has not only dedicated her anthology to Harry but she believes that he has helped her to write it. 'For it is the act of constant remembrance that keeps the dead person alive forever. He is there all the time,' she writes, 'and so to talk to him and about him is just the most normal natural instinct... . There is a balance to be found for a grieving person between having the door of communications slammed shut, and talking on obsessively for twenty-four hours a day.'

Having found a sensitive and sympathetic way of counselling bereaved parents and others, taking it to a deeper level, might not the inspiration for the book, which is apparently all about 'leaving the door ajar', be coming from the other side of life itself? The eminent scientist Sir Oliver Lodge, communicating from the other side on the 'two worlds', is reported to have emphatically declared:

We have split up life into two parts far too drastically. We have drawn a line, and we must gradually erase that line. We have talked about the spiritual life, and the earth life or the physical life. The two are one and we must make them one again. There is no line, there is no line at all. Man has drawn a line and it must be erased, and it will take some time to erase it completely, but we must work towards that. We must do that in the same way that we must erase – shall we call it national boundaries? – national boundaries and limitations, racial ones.

All these must go, and especially the boundary that we have, quite unnecessarily, erected between what we now call our two worlds, which are one.[14]

Arthur Conan Doyle, famous author and creator of the detective Sherlock Holmes, was originally a doctor who, in his later years, became increasingly interested in psychic phenomena. In his book *The New Revelation And The Vital Message*, he suggests that, when a young man, and others like him, pass over and return giving proofs of accuracy as to their survival (as reported in his book), we are bound to take their assertions, as to the life they are now leading, very seriously. He then epitomises what these assertions are:

They say they are exceedingly happy, and that they do not wish to return. They are among the friends whom they had loved and lost, who meet them when they die and continue their careers together. They are very busy on all forms of congenial work. The world in which they find themselves is very much like that which they have quitted, but everything keyed to a higher octave. As in a higher octave the rhythm is the same, and the relation of notes to each other the same, but the total effect different, so it is here.

Conan Doyle continues in more detail with evidence gathered as to the nature of life on the other side:

In its larger issues this happy life to come consists in the development of those gifts which we possess. There is action for the man of action, intellectual work for the thinker, artistic, literary, dramatic and religious for those whose God-given powers lie that way. What we have both in brain and character we carry over with us. No man is too old to learn, for what he learns he keeps. There is no physical side to love and no child-birth, though there is close union between those married people who really love each other, and, generally, there is deep sympathetic friendship and comradeship between the sexes. Every man or woman finds a soul mate sooner or later. The child grows up to the normal, so that the mother who lost a babe of two years old, and dies herself twenty years later finds a grown-up daughter of twenty-two awaiting her coming. Age, which is produced chiefly by the mechanical presence of lime in our arteries, disappears, and the individual reverts to the full normal growth and appearance of completed man – or womanhood.[15]

Although the language of the above extract is rather different to our modern-day terminology – it was first published in 1918 – a strong point in centuries of evidence gathered on every aspect of the afterlife is the similarity of content.

I am not religious. I think I am level-headed and I work as a legal secretary. Two years ago my father-in-law was extremely ill with cancer. For the last eight days of his life my husband and I stayed with him almost continuously and he died holding our hands. No one close to me had ever died before and this affected me deeply. Since his death I have felt him near every day but could only see him as he was when he died, which was extremely distressing.

In October last year his brother L was also dying of cancer. My husband and I went out for a ride on the motor bike. Coming home it was about 6.25 p.m. and almost completely dark. We came up over a hill and I had an extremely strange feeling. I looked over towards the fields and there was a brilliant blue light, dark blue but bright. The sky was blue. It's hard to describe the colour. I am not sure whether I imagined it in my mind but I don't think so: I saw in amongst the blue my late father-in-law's face, a very peaceful face. I then felt his brother die and come to him. It was very peaceful. We must have passed this spot in a matter of seconds but it seemed like minutes. Incidentally, this blue sky highlighted three bare trees, which stood out.

When we got to my mother's house at about 6.30 p.m. I got off the bike and announced to my husband, mother and father that L had just died. Whether it was because of the way I said it or the way I acted, surprisingly, no one laughed and they believed me. We then waited for the telephone to ring to announce his death. At 8 p.m. the call came and the timing was exactly right: he had died when I saw what I have described above right to the minute. Discussing it later, the spot where I had experienced this was in a direct line with the house in which he died.

From that day on I can now see my father-in-law as he was and not the man I had seen dying.[16]

The similarity of evidence; a bright light; remembering every detail; no sense of fear; the 'never-to-be-forgotten experience' – evidence that comes with the following recipient wishing fervently that she had had some religion to help her during a difficult time in her life.

> I was twenty-five and living in a hostel. On a Saturday afternoon I was lying on my bed feeling depressed and lonely. Although I wanted to get up and go out to buy some cigarettes, I felt unable to move because of the feeling of depression. Instead, I continued to lie on the bed and began to wish fervently and with all my strength that I had some religion to help me. Within a few minutes a very bright light appeared in the opposite corner of the room near to the ceiling and I heard a voice say 'Take up your bed and walk.'

> I am a graduate, married now to a scientist, and have never suffered from hallucinations of any sort. I am still not particularly religious, but this experience has stayed with me in complete detail for over thirty years.[17]

Whatever the circumstances, we don't know how, or when, the comforting will come. A mother and daughter and her husband were dreading returning to the family home having stayed away for a few days after the funeral of her father. Entering the house with trepidation, they each walked around silently, lost in their own thoughts, until finally the daughter exclaimed, 'What a wonderful feeling there is in here.' Her mother and husband had had the same feeling, and on discussing it, all agreed it was as if there had been a party in the house.

To repeat the words of a Catholic Priest: 'We don't know how, or when, the comforting will come, it's a matter of faith that

God's love is so great – but a struggling for anything will not go unrewarded.'

• • •

Emily was sixty-six when she learned that her aunt, aged eighty-four years, was a cancer victim, and she was appalled at the thought of having to nurse her. 'Now retired, I was even to devote myself entirely to my nursing duties, which were to last for three months.' Emily tells us her story:

> One night I had settled my patient for the night and sat down in my chair near her bed, with my back to the window. Why, I do not know, but my eyes seemed drawn to the corner of the room. There, at the top of the wall shone a small light, which slowly grew in size and brilliance. I could not withdraw my gaze but I had no sense of fear. I determined to be quite practical and made myself look out of the window, thinking that an outside light might be reflected in the bedroom, but there was no outside light. I sat down again and kept my eyes on the light. I have never, before or after, felt such a sense of peace and comfort. I felt a powerful presence in the bedroom and I knew that I would be given divine strength to carry on with my duty to the end. I felt an exhilaration, a peace and well-being and I knew that I had been given a manifestation of God's care for me, unworthy though I was. I went to sleep, calm and reassured, knowing that the burden was no longer mine.

> There was an unexpected sequel to my experience. On the following night, when I had again attended to my patient, I noticed that she did not, as usual, close her

eyes. I followed her gaze and was surprised to realise that she was staring up at the very place where the light had shone for me. I asked my aunt what she was looking at. She replied, 'Nothing.'

I said, 'Come on. Tell me. What do you see up there?' She replied, 'I'm not going to tell you. It's a secret.'

My aunt died a few days later. I am convinced that we were both, however unworthy, privileged to be granted this manifestation of divine help in our hour of need.[18]

May Walker tells us of her experience when she had given little, if any, thought to spiritual matters, being busy bringing up a family. 'I suppose I would have been classed as an agnostic.' The death of her mother, however, made her begin to search for some deeper meaning to life.

I remember passing the library in the town I was living in at the time and felt compelled, almost pushed in. I had never been a member of a library and read very little. I joined there and then and walked straight to the section on philosophy / comparative religions, etc. I became an avid reader of books on the incarnation, karma and out-of-body experiences. I spent all my spare time reading and learning to meditate. It was at this time that I had my experience.

I was sitting in the dentist's chair waiting for the dentist to examine my teeth. I was alone and looking out of the window. It was a dull, overcast day, but suddenly the sun came out – golden and glorious. This was not the physical sun, but a wonderful golden light. With it came a feeling of great joy, peace and well-being. I was so full of love for all things that I felt my heart would burst, and such a feeling of Unity. I was aware of a hand holding the whole world in its care – regardless of race, colour or creed – this was God caring for all his children. I felt that had I been at home I could have prolonged it, but it faded and the dentist came in and life went on, but never quite the same after.

I couldn't think what had happened to me or why it should have happened to me, but it has been my anchor ever since. It loses so much in the telling, of course. I have never doubted since that day that there is a God and that he is a God of Love. This is not to say that my search has ended, it is still going on, but I feel that it was given as a gift to encourage me to keep on.[19]

Dr Elizabeth Kubler-Ross was a psychiatrist whose work with terminally ill children, Aids patients, and the elderly, proved to her the certainty of life after death. Her books on the subject and her special study of near-death experiences have made her famous throughout the world, and have brought comfort and hope to millions of people. In her own words, she tells us that until she started her work, 'I had absolutely no belief in an afterlife.' At her workshops on death and transition, observers reported that she talked with simplicity and certainty, her vision of the truth borne out by the documented accounts of many people who have had near-death experiences. 'At the moment of death,' she says, 'you pass from the physical realm where you leave your poor old chrysalis. Your butterfly is born and travels towards an incandescent light where those who have loved you and preceded you in death will be waiting. You will be whole again, able to be anywhere with the speed of your thoughts and all knowledge will be yours.'[20]

Her work on the near-death experience led her, in her book *The Wheel of Life*, to write:

> Not only were we told that the death experience was free of pain; people reported that they did not want to come back. After being met by loved ones, or guides, they travelled to a place that was so loving and comforting that they did not want to return. They had to be talked into it. 'It's not time,' was something practically everyone heard. I remember watching a five-year-old boy draw a picture in an effort to explain to his mother how pleasant his death experience had been. First he drew a brightly coloured castle and said, 'This is where God lives.' Then he added a brilliant star. 'When I saw the star, it said, "Welcome Home." '

Kubler-Ross continues, explaining that people describe 'passing' as entering what has commonly been described as a tunnel, or a transitional gate, a bridge, a mountain pass, a pretty stream:

> As their guides took them closer, they felt the light radiating intense warmth, energy, spirit and love. Love most of all. Unconditional love. People reported that its force was overwhelming. They felt excitement, peace, tranquillity, and the anticipation of finally 'going home'.[21]

Experiences, experiences, experiences; we are told that everything happens for a reason. Emma tells us what happened when she arrived home for the funeral of her father:

My father, a Church of England Priest had died. I arrived home for the funeral, and my mother told me my father was laid out in his coffin in the dining room if I would like to see him before he was taken over to the church. I entered the room and was at once hit by a 'singing silence', almost as if Angels were beating their wings and busying themselves with my father's soul. The force was so strong I fell to my knees at the wonder of it all. I now had the proof I longed for, there was something beyond the self. I prayed and left the room.

The day after my father's funeral, I attended communion with my family and a large congregation of parishioners. At the altar rail, with tears streaming down my face, I thought, 'Daddy, where are you? Such a good man, with a strong faith such as yours, are you just snuffed out, was your life, and those of countless other priests just a waste of time?'

Suddenly, a voice so loud I turned round, said, 'I am here, I always said we didn't go anywhere.' He always called me 'worldly Mary, his doubting Thomas'. From that day I have prayed and attended communion regularly.

I don't doubt, I know.[22]

Four months after her husband aged sixty-three died, Alice Parker was reading in bed:

Suddenly I saw him. Not as he had died, old and rather defeated, but youthful, glowing, vibrant. Only head and shoulders appeared, but his hair and face were golden with a great brightness and his eyes were ablaze with an intensity of love that was not human as we know it. In a flash I knew that anything that had happened between us in the way of argument, hard feelings, or dissent, was all wiped out. It had just gone, and did not matter at all. From then on, I was never able to grieve or feel remorse for not having 'done better' on the occasions that come to my mind.

Since then, I have never been able to grieve for him but only to feel happy as the 'vision-transfiguration', call it what you will, is as clear as when it first happened. I feel the vibrant, glowing health, all knowledge, all forgiveness and all joy and power my husband had, seemed to be transmitted to me, and I have been able to adjust and make a contented life for myself.[23]

The search for a deeper meaning to life, for an 'awareness', a realisation that perhaps we are, after all, more than this physical body we inhabit, will take us over many highways and byways and possibly through ions of time; but it would appear that we all have, at one stage or another in life, an opportunity to accept or reject this amazing philosophy. Our opportunity may come through a dream, or it could be simply a strange feeling that brings us awareness. The daughter of a famous footballer describes her feeling as she lay on the bed with him as he was dying:

At 6.30 a.m. just as he was about to pass I felt a great surge of energy pass right through me. It was an amazing and a wonderful feeling and I like to believe it was his soul passing through me.[24]

Jan, visibly grieving at her son's funeral: the other mourners, during the tea after the service, were astounded to see her suddenly peaceful and having a little smile to herself. It was only to a close friend she confided the reason. Jan suddenly knew her son was saying to her, 'Mam, mam, don't be so silly.' A strong smell of tobacco smoke as she cleaned out the kitchen cupboard told Vanessa that her dad who had died was near; because of a strong thought that he acted on immediately Alan was able to be with his mother during her last moments.

Our 'opportunity' doesn't have to come through some dramatic revelation. It may come, as Alan's did, through a thought; it could come through a feeling; a serious illness; a tragedy; a chance meeting; the loss of a loved one; the break-up of a relationship, a psychic experience, a spiritual experience; an unexpected act of kindness, a sudden upliftment; an answer to prayer. All part of God's magic? A seed sown, or a spark that will ignite a flame...or just one of those things.

Having experienced the experience, having even a tiny part of our mind made receptive, with the door ajar, the decision is ours. Do we go on creating barriers of disbelief, wanting more proof, then demanding yet more proof? If we demand, however, we are told to remember, 'a closed mind will never find it'. We become aware but then close the door. Wanting evidence, wanting to be absolutely assured? With a closed mind, we never will be convinced but when the pupil is ready, the teacher will appear:

> the death of her mother made her begin to search for some deeper meaning to life; 'I remember passing the library in the town I was living in at the time and felt compelled, almost pushed in...

It would seem, however, that no one religion or philosophy has all the answers and, therefore, only some of the truth (O deepest mystery); but perhaps each and every one of us, in one way or another, have been 'touched' by the 'unnamed something', the 'universal energy', the 'life force', 'God', as was the writer in the following account, who tries to explain the experience.

Something came to me when I was thirteen years old. I saw a picture of a pile of Jews' bodies waiting to be bulldozed into a mass grave in Germany during the Second World War. Of course I was shocked, but the 'whatever it is' took the opportunity to pound my brain from the inside for twelve hours. I can remember thinking, 'I don't know what you want. What am I to do?' I was not confused or frightened, just sort of 'taken over'. At the end of the twelve hours I thought – though I can't remember why – that maybe I should choose a career as a doctor. Suddenly the 'whatever it is' vacated my head and allowed me to return to normal.

That was it really. People were a bit surprised at my career choice, because I was rather a 'slow starter'. I plodded a bit harder with school work, but not really enough to justify the sharp increase in success I experienced at O level. I had a minor set-back when one of my A-level grades was too low for entry to medical school, but it was only a temporary loss of confidence. 'Whatever it is' can cope with well-intentioned plodders apparently, and I got in the next year.

I used to wonder if this thing that gives me strength had some sort of mission for me. I doubt this, as despite a certain knowledge that God exists, I cannot find him/her in religion of any sort (not that I've tried very much). In fact, I prefer not to think about it at all in case it goes away. It's nice not to have to worry about bad times. 'It' arrives when necessary, sometimes in the most unexpected situations.[25]

The comment has been made recently (by a believer), 'Why cannot we be as passionate about our spirituality as a rock star about his music or a footballer about his game?' But then another comment, also made recently, by a man who had studied various religions, and was desperately seeking enlightenment , suggests that 'too deep and serious a study of spirituality can become too intellectual and take the heart out of it'. We miss the message:

> I hadn't been brought up with much faith, and I can truly say I was at the bottom of a black pit. Kneeling by my son's cot in great anguish, I suddenly seemed to be surrounded by, and filled with light and warmth and incredible peace.

• • •

And so it is that often, through a humble, quick-as-a-flash unexplainable experience, true understanding is reached; the truth of the words 'unconditional love' realised, and a life changed, never to be the same again.

One experience, countless experiences, every experience it seems, beams out the same message of 'love'. Unconditional love, pure and true, transcending all religions and creeds, colour and circumstance and bearing with it a message of 'hope'; of an ever-present help in times of trouble reaching out to us through the seemingly 'impossible', the 'bizarre', the ordinary; assuring us that, no matter what the situation, our need can be met. It is a message of the continuity of life, of all life, in its many facets; here, now, interacting with us all the time; not on another level or plain but surrounding us 'as it was in the beginning'; the universe a harmonious whole, the two worlds one.

It would appear, however, that the onus is on we ourselves to be 'aware', 'receptive', 'sensitive', alive to this constant, never ending flow of energy/love that surrounds us, ours for the taking.

> It's nice not to have to worry about bad times. 'It' arrives when necessary, sometimes in the most unexpected situations.

Through prayer/thought, tuning in, keeping the door open, asking, thanking, acknowledging – Uliana Lopatkina, the principal ballerina with the Kirov in St Petersburg acknowledges

> the spiritual condition of a ballerina is as important as her physique. I never dance just with my body.[26]

– acknowledging that, strange as it may seem, with all our faults and foibles, rough edges and eccentricities, we are, all of us, spirit here and now, inhabiting a physical body.

• • •

Right now, we consider the innumerable so-called 'paranormal' experiences that have manifested themselves over the centuries, throughout history, throughout the many and varied religions of the world; paranormal experiences that have occurred in the humblest of situations, in everyday life; and as we try to understand that therefore earliest man also received guidance and help from the 'It', 'the unnamed something', 'God'; guidance and help which was as relevant to him in his day as our experiences are to us today, we can perhaps appreciate more fully the words of the Rev W H Elliott, Domestic Chaplain to King George VI, who wrote, in a little book entitled, *Can I Help You?*

Nothing has been changed. If there was an unseen world then, there is an unseen world now. It is we who have changed, we who have lost the power of seeing or even of believing that anything is there but the material stuff of which we make our life. But it *is* there.

And right now, can we also consider a most thought-provoking fact? If one, and only one, of all the experiences we have ever read about in books or newspapers or magazines, or heard about on the radio, through film, or on the internet – experiences that have been related to us personally, or experiences that we have perhaps been privileged to witness for ourselves – if one, and only one, of all these experiences, if ONE and only ONE, of ALL THE EXPERIENCES THE WORLD HAS EVER KNOWN is proved to be true, then that is all the evidence needed to establish that there is indeed 'something', something after so-called death. Proof?... consider it, only one experience!

Maybe the party isn't over after all; perhaps it has just begun.

References

* The Religious Experience Research Centre, University of Wales, Ceredigion, will be referred to as RERC in the following chapters.

INTRODUCTION

1   John Keeble, *This Unnamed Something, A Personal Portrait of the Life of Professor Sir Alister Hardy FRS 1896 – 1985*, RERC
2   Billy Graham, *Angels*, p.12

CHAPTER ONE

1   RERC (1131)
2   *Daily Mirror*, 15th July 2005
3   *Sunday Times*, July 2002
4   RERC (003627)

CHAPTER TWO

1   Ivor Novella, *The Dancing Years*
2   Hugh Lynn Cayce, Tom C Clark, *Dreams*
3   Shane Miller, William N Peterson
4   RERC (002733)
5   RERC (002725)

6   RERC (003356)
7   Roman missal for the dead, Preface I
8   Shakespeare, *Hamlet*
9   Billy Graham, *Angels*

CHAPTER THREE

1   Hebrews 13 v 2
2   Billy Graham, *Angels*, p.32
3   Matthew 11 v 25
4   RERC (4644)
5   RERC
6   Billy Graham, *Angels*, p.30
7   RERC (003622)
8   RERC (003649)
9   RERC (00146)
10   RERC (2602)
11   RERC (002704)
12   RERC
13   RERC (062738)
14   Reiki Healing: Reiki is the Japanese word for Universal Life
     Energy. REI meaning universal, i.e. that it is present
     everywhere. KI is the Life Force, a non-physical energy that
     flows through all living things. It is an ancient energy healing
     system rediscovered in the late nineteenth century by a
     Japanese scholar Dr Mikao Usui.
15   RERC (003355)
16   RERC (4644)
17   RERC (003396)
18   RERC (003608)
19   RERC (003616)
20   George Gallup, Jr, *Adventures in Immortality*, p.91
21   George Gallup, Jr, *Adventures in Immortality*, p.94

22   RERC (003338)

23   Daniel 10 v18-19

24   Exodus 23 v20

25   Acts 12 v10

26   Billy Graham, *Angels*, p11

CHAPTER FOUR

1   Ralph Waldo Trine, *In Tune With The Infinite*, p.v

2   RERC

3   RERC (003336)

4   RERC (002735)

5   Brenda Maddox, *April Blood*. p.244

6   RERC (24)

7   Genesis 12 v1

8   *Sunday Times Style Magazine* – 2004

9   RERC (900362)

10   BBC2 *Heart of the Matter*, Oct 2003 'Does Prayer Work?'

11   RERC (003327)

12   Air Chief Marshal Lord Dowding 'God's Magic' p.18

13   George Gallup, Jr, *Adventures in Immortality*, p.16

14   George Braden newsletter 48 summer 2004 – The Edgar
      Cayce Centre, Durham

15   George Gallup, Jr, *Adventures in Immortality*, p.16

16   RERC (2062)

17   George Gallup, Jr, *Adventures in Immortality*, p.17

18   RERC (4092)

19   RERC (2524)

20   RERC (2526)

21   RERC (1136)

22   RERC (2568)

23   *Times Magazine*, Aug 2004 'Life in the day of'
      RaHimullah Kabul, Afghanistan

CHAPTER FIVE

1   Ralph Waldo Trine, *In Tune With The Infinite*, p.31
2   Air Chief Marshal Lord Dowding, *God's Magic*, p.56
3   *Psychic News* 2004
4   RERC   archive 9
5   RERC (1448)
6   Dennis Borders' 'Psychic Animals'
7   BBC1, *Dangerous Passions*, May 2004
8   RERC
9   RERC (2138)
10 RERC (4261)
11 RERC (2611)
12 RERC (4278)
13 RERC (4614)
14 RERC (4182)
15 RERC (2674)
16 RERC (1637)
17 RERC (606240)

CHAPTER SEVEN

1   *Daily Mail*, June 2004
2   James Hamilton, *Farraday, The Life*, p.222
3   Gijs van Hensbergen, *Gaudi*, p.104
4   *Sunday Times Magazine* 2004, from an entry in a diary kept by Patti Davis, President Reagan's daughter, at the time of his passing.
5   Philip Norman, *Shout*, p.143
6   RERC   archive 196
7   RERC (1679)
8   RERC (002533)
9   RERC (002715)

10   RERC (000517)

11   George Gallup, Jr, *Adventures in Immortality*, p.14

12   Ecclesiastes 3, v1, 2

13   Harry Scott poem, 'Death is nothing at all'

14   Paul Beard, *Living On*, pub 1980, p.194

15   *Arthur Conan Doyle, The New Revelation and the Vital Message*, pub Psychic Press Ltd, p.122-123

16   RERC (4057)

17   RERC (4410)

18   RERC (2026)

19   RERC (43840

20   Allegra Taylor, *I Fly Out with Bright Feathers* (The Quest of a Novice Healer), p.56

21   Elizabeth Kubler-Ross, *The Wheel of Life*, p.188-190

22   RERC (001550)

23   RERC (004323)

24   BBC4 April 2005, *Tribute to Bobby Moore*

25   RERC (4110)

26   *Sunday Times Magazine* 2005, 'A Life in the day of'